The Fascist Offensive and the Tasks of the Communist International in the Struggle of the
Working Class against Fascism by Georgi Dimitrov
First Prism Key Press Edition 2012

Prism Key Press
New York, NY 10001
PrismKeyPress.com

ISBN-13: 978-1475029611

The Fascist Offensive

And the Tasks of the Communist International in the Struggle of the Working Class against Fascism

Georgi Dimitrov

CONTENTS

I. FASCISM AND THE WORKING CLASS

Comrades, as early as the Sixth Congress [1928], the Communist International warned the world proletariat that a new fascist offensive was under way and called for a struggle against it. The Congress pointed out that 'in a more or less developed form, fascist tendencies and the germs of a fascist movement are to be found almost everywhere.'

With the development of the very deep economic crisis, with the general crisis of capitalism becoming sharply accentuated and the mass of working people becoming revolutionized, fascism has embarked upon a wide offensive. The ruling bourgeoisie more and more seeks salvation in fascism, with the object of taking exceptional predatory measures against the working people, preparing for an imperialist war of plunder, attacking the Soviet Union, enslaving and partitioning China, and by all these means preventing revolution.

The imperialist circles are trying to shift the *whole* burden of the crisis onto the shoulders of the working people. *That is why they need fascism.*

They are trying to solve the problem of markets by enslaving the weak nations, by intensifying colonial oppression and repartitioning the world anew by means of war. *That is why they need fascism.*

They are striving to *forestall* the growth of the forces of revolution by smashing the revolutionary movement of the workers and peasants and by undertaking a military attack against the Soviet Union -- the bulwark of the world proletariat. *That is why they need fascism.*

In a number of countries, Germany in particular, these imperialist circles have succeeded, *before* the masses had decisively turned towards revolution, in inflicting defeat on the proletariat, and establishing a fascist dictatorship.

But it is characteristic of the victory of fascism that this victory, on the one hand, bears witness to the weakness of the proletariat, disorganized and paralyzed by the disruptive Social-Democratic policy of class collaboration with the bourgeoisie, and, on the other, expresses the weakness of the bourgeoisie itself, afraid of the realization of a united struggle of the working class, afraid of revolution, and no longer in a position to maintain its dictatorship over the masses by the old methods of bourgeois democracy and parliamentarism.

The class character of fascism

Comrades, fascism in power was correctly described by the Thirteenth Plenum of the Executive Committee of the Communist International *as the open terrorist dictatorship of the most reactionary, most chauvinistic and most imperialist elements of finace capital.*

The most reactionary variety of fascism is the *German type* of fascism. It has the effrontery to call itself National Socialism, though it has nothing in common with socialism. German fascism is not only bourgeois nationalism, it is fiendish chauvinism. It is a government system of political gangsterism, a system of provocation and torture practised upon the working class and the revolutionary elements of the peasantry, the petty bourgeoisie and the intelligentsia. It is medieval barbarity and bestiality, it is unbridled aggression in relation to other nations.

German fascism is acting *as the spearhead of international counter-revolution, as the chief instigator of imperialist war, as the initiator of a crusade against the Soviet Union, the great fatherland of the working people of the whole world.*

Fascism is not a form of state power "standing above both classes -- the proletariat and the bourgeoisie," as Otto Bauer, for instance, has asserted. It is not "the revolt of the petty bourgeoisie which has captured the machinery of the state," as the British Socialist Brailsford declares. No, fascism is not a power standing above class, nor government of the petty bourgeoisie or the *lumpen-proletariat* over finance capital. Fascism is the power of finance capital itself. It is the organization of terrorist vengeance against the working class and the revolutionary section of the peasantry and intelligentsia. In foreign policy, fascism is jingoism in its most brutal form, fomenting bestial hatred of other nations.

This, the true character of fascism, must be particularly stressed because in a number of countries, under cover of social demagogy, fascism has managed to gain the following of the mass of the petty bourgeoisie that has been dislocated by the crisis, and even of certain sections of the most backward strata of the proletariat. These would never have supported fascism if they had understood its real character and its true nature.

The development of fascism, and the fascist dictatorship itself, assume *different forms* in different countries, according to historical, social and economic conditions and to the national peculiarities, and the international position of the given country. In certain countries, principally those in which fascism has no broad mass basis and in which the struggle of the various groups within the camp of the fascist bourgeoisie itself is rather acute, fascism does not immediately venture to abolish parliament, but allows the other bourgeois parties, as well as the Social-Democratic Parties, to retain a modicum of legality. In other countries, where the ruling bourgeoisie fears an *early* outbreak of revolution, fascism establishes its unrestricted political monopoly, either immediately or by intensifying its reign of terror against and persecution of all rival parties and groups. This does not prevent fascism, when its position becomes *particularly* acute, from trying to extend its basis and, without altering its class nature, trying *to combine* open terrorist dictatorship with a crude sham of parliamentarism.

The accession to power of fascism is not an *ordinary succession* of one bourgeois government by another, but a *substitution* of one state form of class domination of the bourgeoisie -- bourgeois democracy -- by another form -- open terrorist dictatorship. It would be a serious mistake to ignore this distinction, a mistake liable to prevent the revolutionary proletariat from mobilizing the widest strata of the working people of town and country for the struggle against the menace of the seizure of power by the fascists, and from taking advantage of the contradictions which exist in the camp of the bourgeoisie itself. But it is a mistake, no less serious and dangerous, to *underrate* the importance, for the establishment of fascist dictatorship, of the *reactionary measures of the bourgeoisie at present increasingly developing in bourgeois-democratic* countries -- measures which suppress the democratic liberties of the working people, falsify and curtail the rights of parliament and intensify the repression of the revolutionary movement.

Comrades, the accession to power of fascism must not be conceived of in so simplified and smooth a form, as though some committee or other of finance capital decided on a certain date to set up a fascist dictatorship. In reality, fascism usually comes to power in the course of a mutual, and at times severe, struggle against the old bourgeois parties, or a definite section of these parties, in the course of a struggle even within the fascist camp itself -- a struggle which at times leads to armed clashes, as we have witnessed in the case of Germany, Austria and other countries. All this, however, does not make less important the fact that, before the establishment of a fascist dictatorship, bourgeois governments usually pass through a number of preliminary stages and adopt a number of reactionary measures which directly facilitate the accession to power of fascism. Whoever does not fight the reactionary measures of the bourgeoisie and the growth of fascism at these preparatory stages *is not in a position to prevent the victory of fascism, but, on the contrary, facilitates that victory.*

The Social-Democratic leaders glossed over and concealed from the masses the true class nature of fascism, and did not call them to the struggle against the increasingly reactionary measures of the bourgeoisie. They bear great

13

historical responsibility for the fact that, at the decisive moment of the fascist offensive, a large section of the working people of Germany and of a number of other fascist countries failed to recognize in fascism the most bloodthirsty monster of finance capital, their most vicious enemy, and that these masses were not prepared to resist it.

What is the source of the influence of fascism over the masses? Fascism is able to attract the masses because it demagogically appeals to their *most urgent needs and demands.* Fascism not only inflames prejudices that are deeply ingrained in the masses, but also plays on the better sentiments of the masses, on their sense of justice and sometimes even on their revolutionary traditions. Why do the German fascists, those lackeys of the bourgeoisie and mortal enemies of socialism, represent themselves to the masses as "Socialists," and depict their accession to power as a "revolution"? Because they try to exploit the faith in revolution and the urge towards socialism that lives in the hearts of the mass of working people in Germany.

Fascism acts in the interests of the extreme imperialists, but it presents itself to the masses in the guise of champion of an ill-treated nation, and appeals to outraged national sentiments, as German fascism did, for instance, when it won the support of the masses of the petty bourgeoisie by the slogan "Down with the Versailles Treaty."

Fascism aims at the most unbridled exploitation of the masses but it approaches them with the most artful anti-capitalist demagogy, taking advantage of the deep hatred of the working people against the plundering bourgeoisie, the banks, trusts and financial magnates, and advancing those slogans which at the given moment are most alluring to the politically immature masses. In Germany -- "The general welfare is higher than the welfare of the individual," in Italy -- "Our state is not a capitalist, but a corporate state," in Japan -- "For Japan without

14

exploitation," in the United States -- "Share the wealth," and so forth.

Fascism delivers up the people to be devoured by the most corrupt and venal elements, but comes before them with the demand for "an honest and incorruptible government." Speculating on the profound disillusionment of the masses in bourgeois-democratic governments, fascism hypocritically denounces corruption.

It is in the interests of the most reactionary circles of the bourgeoisie that fascism intercepts the disappointed masses who desert the old bourgeois parties. But it impresses these masses by the *vehemence of its attacks* on the bourgeois governments and its irreconcilable attitude to the old bourgeois parties.

Surpassing in its cynicism and hypocrisy all other varieties of bourgeois reaction, fascism *adapts* its demagogy to the national *peculiarities* of each country, and even to the peculiarities of the various social strata in one and the same country. And the mass of the petty bourgeoisie and even a section of the workers, reduced to despair by want, unemployment and the insecurity of their existence, fall victim to the social and chauvinist demagogy of fascism.

Fascism comes to power as a *party of attack* on the revolutionary movement of the proletariat, on the mass of the people who are in a state of unrest; yet it stages its accession to power as a "revolutionary" movement against the bourgeoisie on behalf of "the whole nation" and for the "salvation" of the nation. One recalls Mussolini's "march" on Rome, Pilsudski's "march" on Warsaw, Hitler's National-Socialist "revolution" in Germany, and so forth.

But whatever the masks that fascism adopts, whatever the forms in which it presents itself, whatever the ways by which it comes to power

- *Fascism is a most ferocious attack by capital on*

15

the mass of the working people;

• *Fascism is unbridled chauvinism and predatory war;*

• *Fascism is rabid reaction and counter-revolution;*

• *Fascism is the most vicious enemy of the working class and of all working people.*

What does fascist victory bring to the masses?

Fascism promised the workers "a fair wage," but actually it has brought them an even lower, a pauper, standard of living. It promised work for the unemployed, but actually it has brought them even more painful torments of starvation and forced servile labor. In practice it converts the workers and unemployed into pariahs of capitalist society stripped of rights; destroys their trade unions; deprives them of the right to strike and to have their working-class press, forces them into fascist organizations, plunders their social insurance funds and transforms the mills and factories into barracks where the unbridled arbitrary rule of the capitalist reigns.

Fascism promised the working youth a broad highway to a brilliant future. But actually it has brought wholesale dismissals of young workers, labor camps and incessant military drilling for a war of conquest.

Fascism promised to guarantee *office workers, petty officials* and *intellectuals* security of existence, to destroy the omnipotence of the trusts and wipe out profiteering by bank capital. But actually it has brought them an ever greater degree of despair and uncertainty as to the morrow; it is subjecting them to a new bureaucracy made up of the most submissive of its followers, it is setting up an intolerable dictatorship of the trusts and spreading corruption and degeneration to an unprecedented extent.

Fascism promised the ruined and impoverished peasants to put an end to debt bondage, to abolish rent and even to expropriate the landed estates without compensation, in the interests of the landless and ruined peasants. But actually it is placing the laboring peasants in a state of unprecedented servitude to the trusts and the fascist state apparatus, and pushes to the utmost limit the exploitation of the great mass of the peasantry by the big landowners, the banks and the usurers.

"Germany will be a peasant country, or will not be at all," Hitler solemnly declared. And what did the peasants of Germany get under Hitler? The moratorium, [1] which has already been cancelled? Or the law on the inheritance of peasant property, which leads to millions of sons and daughters of peasants being squeezed out of the villages and reduced to paupers? Farm laborers have been transformed into semi-serfs, deprived even of the elementary right of free movement. The working peasants have been deprived of the opportunity of selling the produce of their farms in the market.

And in Poland?

The Polish peasant, says the Polish newspaper *Czas*, employs methods and means Which were used perhaps only in the Middle Ages; he nurses the fire in his stove and lends it to his neighbor; he splits matches into several parts; he lends dirty soapwater to others; he boils herring barrels in order to obtain salt water. This is not a fable, but the actual state of affairs in the countryside, of the truth of which anybody may convince himself.

And it is not Communists who write this, Comrades, but a Polish reactionary newspaper.

But this is by no means all.

Every day, in the concentration camps of fascist Germany, in the cellars of the Gestapo (German secret police), in the torture chambers of Poland, in the cells of the Bulgarian and Finnish secret police, in the *Glavnyacha* in Belgrade, in the Rumanian *Siguranza* and on the Italian islands, the best sons of the working class, revolutionary peasants, fighters for the splendid future of mankind, are being subjected to revolting tortures and indignities, before which pale the most abominable acts of the tsarist *Okhranka* [2]. The blackguardly German fascists beat husbands to a bloody pulp in the presence of their wives, and send the ashes of murdered sons by parcel post to their mothers. Sterilization has been made a method of political warfare. In the torture chambers, imprisoned anti-fascists are given injections of poison, their arms are broken, their eyes gouged out; they are strung up and have water pumped into them; the fascist swastika is carved in their living flesh.

I have before me a statistical summary drawn up by the International Red Aid *[international organization of that time for aid to revolutionary fighters]* regarding the number of killed, wounded, arrested, maimed and tortured to death in Germany, Poland, Italy, Austria, Bulgaria and Yugoslavia. In Germany alone, since the National-Socialists came to power, over 4,200 anti-fascist workers, peasants, employees, intellectuals -- Communists, Social Democrats and members of opposition Christian organizations -- have been murdered, 317,800 arrested, 218,600 injured and subjected to torture. In Austria, since the battles of February last year the "Christian" fascist government has murdered 1,900 revolutionary workers, maimed and injured 10,000 and arrested 40,000. And this summary, comrades is far from complete.

Words fail me in describing the indignation which seizes us at the thought of the torments which the working people are now undergoing in a number of fascist countries. The facts and figures we quote do not reflect *one hundredth part of the true picture* of the exploitation and tortures inflicted by the White terror and forming part of the daily life of the working class in many capitalist countries. Volumes cannot give a just picture of the countless brutalities inflicted by fascism on the working people.

With feelings of profound emotion and hatred for the

19

fascist butchers, we dip the banners of the Communist International before the unforgettable memory of John Scheer, Fiete Schulze and Luttgens in Germany, Koloman Wallisch and Munichreiter in Austria, Sallai and Furst in Hungary, Kofardjiev, Lyutibrodski and Voykov in Bulgaria -- before the memory of thousands and thousands of Communists, Social-Democrats and non-party workers, peasants and representatives of the progressive intelligentsia who have laid down their lives in the struggle against fascism.

From this platform we greet the leader of the German proletariat and the honorary chairman of our Congress -- Comrade Thaelmann. We greet Comrades Rakosi, Gramsci, Antikainen. We greet Tom Mooney, who has been languishing in prison for eighteen years, and the thousands of other prisoners of capitalism and fascism, and we say to them: "Brothers in the fight, brothers in arms, you are not forgotten. We are with you. We shall give every hour of our lives, every drop of our blood, for your liberation, and for the liberation of all working people from the shameful regime of fascism."

Comrades, it was Lenin who warned us that the bourgeoisie may succeed in overwhelming the working people by savage terror, in checking the growing forces of revolution for brief periods of time, but that, nevertheless, this would not save it from its doom.

Life will assert itself -- Lenin wrote -- Let the bourgeoisie rave, work itself into a frenzy, overdo things, commit stupidities, take vengeance on the Bolsheviks in advance and endeavour to kill off (in India, Hungary, Germany, etc.) hundreds, thousands and hundreds of thousands more of yesterday's and tomorrow's Bolsheviks. Acting thus, the bourgeoisie acts as all classes doomed by history have acted. Communists should know that the future, at any rate, belongs to them; therefore we can and must combine the most intense passion in the great revolutionary struggle with the coolest and most sober evaluation of the mad ravings of the bourgeoisie. *[V. I. Lenin,* **"Left-Wing" Communism: An Infantile Disorder,** *New York (1949), pp. 81-82;* **Collected Works** *31:101]*

Ay, if we and the proletariat of the whole world firmly follow the path indicated by Lenin, the bourgeoisie will perish in spite of everything.

Is the victory of fascism inevitable?

Why was it that fascism could triumph, and how? Fascism is the most vicious enemy of the working class and working people, who constitute nine-tenths of the German people, nine-tenths of the Austrian people, nine-tenths of the people in other fascist countries. How, in what way, could this vicious enemy triumph?

Fascism was able to come to power *primarily* because the working class, owing to the policy of class collaboration with the bourgeoisie pursued by the Social-Democratic leaders, *proved to be split, politically and organizationally disarmed*, in face of the onslaught of the bourgeoisie. And the Communist Parties, on the other hand, apart from and in opposition to the Social-Democrats, *were not strong enough* to rouse the masses and to lead them in a decisive struggle against fascism.

And, indeed, let the millions of Social-Democratic workers, who together with their Communist brothers are now experiencing the horrors of fascist barbarism, seriously reflect on the following: If, in 1918, when revolution broke out in Germany and Austria, the Austrian and German proletariat had not followed the Social Democratic leadership of Otto Bauer, Friedrich Adler and Karl Renner in Austria and Ebert and Scheidemann in Germany, but had followed the road of the Russian Bolsheviks, the road of Lenin, there would now be no fascism in Austria or Germany, in Italy or Hungary, in Poland or in the Balkans. Not the bourgeoisie, but the working class would long ago have been the master of the situation in Europe.

Take, for example, the *Austrian* Social-Democratic Party. The revolution of 1918 raised it to a tremendous height. It held the power in its hands, it held strong j positions in the army and in the state apparatus. Relying on these positions, it could have nipped fascism in the bud. But it surrendered one position of the working class after another without resistance. It allowed the bourgeoisie to strengthen its power, annul the constitution, purge the state apparatus, army and police force of Social-Democratic functionaries, and take the arsenals away from the workers. It allowed the fascist bandits to murder Social-Democratic workers with impunity and accepted the terms of the Hüttenberg Pact [3], which gave the fascist elements entry to the factories. At the same time the Social-Democratic leaders fooled the workers with the Linz program [4], which contained the alternative possibility of using armed force against the bourgeoisie and establishing the proletarian dictatorship, assuring them that in the event of the ruling class using force against the working class, the Party would reply by a call for general strike and for armed struggle. As though the whole policy of preparation for a fascist attack on the working class were not one chain of acts of violence against the working class masked by constitutional forms. Even on the eve and in the course of the February battles the Austrian Social Democratic leaders left the heroically fighting Schutzbund [5] isolated from the broad masses, and doomed the Austrian proletariat to defeat.

Was the victory of fascism inevitable in *Germany?* No, the German working class could have prevented it.

But in order to do so, it should have achieved a united anti-fascist proletarian front, and forced the Social-Democratic leaders to discontinue their campaign against the Communists and to accept the repeated proposals of the Communist Party for united action against fascism.

When fascism was on the offensive and the bourgeois-democratic liberties were being progressively abolished by the bourgeoisie, it should not have contented itself with the verbal resolutions of the Social-Democrats, but should have replied by a genuine mass struggle, which would have made the fulfilment of the fascist plans of the German bourgeoisie more difficult.

It should not have allowed the prohibition of the League of Red Front Fighters by the government of Braun and Severing [6], and should have established fighting contact between the League and the Reichsbanner [7], with its nearly one million members, and should have compelled Braun and Severing to arm both these organizations in order to resist and smash the fascist bands.

It should have compelled the Social-Democratic leaders who headed the Prussian government to adopt measures of defence against fascism, arrest the fascist leaders, close down their press, confiscate their material resources and the resources of the capitalists who were financing the fascist movement, dissolve the fascist organizations, deprive them of their weapons, and so forth.

Furthermore, it should have secured the re-establishment and extension of all forms of social assistance and the introduction of a moratorium and crisis benefits for the peasants -- who were being ruined under the impact of crisis -- by taxing the banks and the trusts, in this way winning the support of the working peasants. It was the fault of the Social-Democrats of Germany that this was not done, and that is why fascism was able to triumph.

Was it inevitable that the bourgeoisie and the aristocracy should have triumphed in Spain, a country where the forces of proletarian revolt are so advantageously combined with a peasant war?

The Spanish Socialists were in the government from the first days of the revolution. Did they establish fighting contact between the working class organizations of every political opinion, including the Communists and the Anarchists, and did they weld the working class into a united trade union organization? Did they demand the confiscation of all lands of the landlords, the church and the monasteries in favor of the peasants in order to win over the latter to the side of the revolution? Did they attempt to fight for national self-determination for the Catalonians and the Basques, and for the liberation of Morocco? Did they purge the army of monarchist and fascist elements and prepare it for passing over to the side of the workers and peasants? Did they dissolve the Civil Guard, so detested by the people, the executioner of every movement of the people? Did they strike at the fascist party of Gil Robles and at the might of the Catholic church? No, they did none of these things. They rejected the frequent proposals of the Communists for united action against the offensive of the bourgeois-landlord reaction and fascism; they passed election laws which enabled the reactionaries to gain a majority in the Cortes (parliament), laws which penalized the popular movement, laws under which the heroic miners of Asturias are now being tried. They had peasants who were fighting for land shot by the Civil Guard, and so on.

This is the way in which the Social-Democrats, by disorganizing and splitting the ranks of the working class, cleared the path to power for fascism in Germany, Austria and Spain.

Comrades, fascism also attained power for the reason that the proletariat found itself isolated from its natural allies. Fascism attained power because it was able to win over *large masses of the peasantry*, owing to the fact that the Social-Democrats in the name of the working class pursued what was in fact an anti-peasant policy. The peasant saw in power a number of Social-Democratic governments, which in his eyes were an embodiment of the power of the working class; but not one of them put an end to peasant want, none of them gave land to the peasantry. In Germany, the Social-Democrats did not touch the landlords; they combated the strikes of the farm laborers, with the result that long before Hitler came to power the farm laborers of Germany were deserting the reformist trade unions and in the majority of cases were going over to the Stahlhelm and to the National Socialists.

Fascism also attained power for the reason that it was able to penetrate into the ranks of the youth, whereas the Social-Democrats diverted the working class youth from the class struggle, while the revolutionary proletariat did not develop the necessary educational work among the youth and did not pay enough attention to the struggle for its specific interests and demands. Fascism grasped the very acute need of the youth for militant activity, and enticed a considerable section of the youth into its fighting detachments. The new generation of young men and women has not experienced the horrors of war. They have felt the full weight of the economic crisis, unemployment and the disintegration of bourgeois democracy. But, seeing no prospects for the future, large sections of the youth proved to be particularly receptive to fascist demagogy, which depicted for them an alluring future should fascism succeed.

In this connection, we cannot avoid referring also to a number of *mistakes made by the Communist Parties*, mistakes that hampered our struggle against fascism.

In our ranks there was an impermissible underestimation of the fascist danger, a tendency which to this day has not everywhere been overcome. A case in point is the opinion formerly to be met with in our Parties that "Germany is not Italy," meaning that fascism may have succeeded in Italy, but that its success in Germany was out of the question, because the latter is an industrially and culturally highly developed country, with forty years of traditions of the working-class movement, in which fascism was impossible. Or the kind of opinion which is to be met with nowadays, to the effect that in countries of "classical" bourgeois democracy the soil for fascism does not exist. Such opinions have served and may serve to relax vigilance towards the fascist danger, and to render the mobilization of the proletariat in the struggle against fascism more difficult.

One might also cite quite a few instances where Communists were taken unawares by the fascist coup. Remember Bulgaria, where the leadership of our Party, took up a "neutral," but in fact opportunist, position with regard to the *coup d'état* of June 9, 1923; Poland, where in May 1926 the leadership of the Communist Party, making a wrong estimate of the motive forces of the Polish revolution, did not realize the fascist nature of Pilsudski's *coup*, and trailed in the rear of events; Finland, where our Party based itself on a false conception of slow and gradual fascization and overlooked the fascist coup which was being prepared by the leading group of the bourgeoisie and which took the Party and the working class unawares.

When National Socialism had already become a menacing mass movement in Germany, there were comrades who regarded the Bruening government as already a government of fascist dictatorship, and who boastfully declared: "If Hitler's Third Reich ever comes about, it will be six feet underground, and above it will be the victorious power of the workers."

Our comrades in Germany for a long time failed to fully reckon with the wounded national sentiments and the indignation of the masses against the Versailles Treaty; they treated as of little account the waverings of the peasantry and petty bourgeoisie; they were late in drawing up their program of social and national emancipation, and when they did put it forward they were unable to adapt it to the concrete demands and to the level of the masses. They were even unable to popularize it widely among the masses.

In a number of countries, the necessary development of a mass fight against fascism was replaced by barren debates on the nature of fascism "in general" and by a narrow sectarian attitude in formulating and solving the immediate political tasks of the Party.

Comrades, it is not simply because we want to dig up the past that we speak of the causes of the victory of fascism, that we point to the historical responsibility of the Social Democrats for the defeat of the working class, and that we also point out our own mistakes in the fight against fascism. We are not historians divorced from living reality; we, active fighters of the working class, are obliged to answer the question that is tormenting millions of workers: *Can the victory of fascism be prevented, and how?* And we reply to these millions of workers: Yes, comrades, the road to fascism can be blocked. It is quite possible. It depends on ourselves-on the workers, the peasants and all working people.

Whether the victory of fascism can be prevented depends *first and foremost* on the militant activity of the working class itself, on whether its forces are welded into a single militant army combating the offensive of capitalism and fascism. By establishing its fighting unity, the proletariat would paralyze the influence of fascism over the peasantry, the urban petty bourgeoisie, the youth and the intelligentsia, and would be able to neutralize one section of them and win over the other section.

Second, it depends on the existence of a strong revolutionary party, correctly leading the struggle of the working people against fascism. A party which systematically calls on the workers to retreat in the face of fascism and permits the fascist bourgeoisie to strengthen its positions is doomed to lead the workers to defeat.

Third, it depends on a correct policy of the working class towards the peasantry and the petty-bourgeois masses of the towns. These masses must be taken as they are, and not as we should like to have them. It is in the process of the struggle that they will overcome their doubts and waverings. It is only by a patient attitude towards their inevitable waverings, it is only by the political help of the proletariat, that they will be able to rise to a higher level of revolutionary consciousness and activity.

Fourth, it depends on the vigilance and timely action of the revolutionary proletariat. The latter must not allow fascism to take it unawares, it must not surrender the initiative to fascism, but must inflict decisive blows on it before it can gather its forces, it must not allow fascism to consolidate its position, it must repel fascism wherever and whenever it rears its head, it must not allow fascism to gain new positions. This is what the French proletariat is so successfully trying to do.

These are the main conditions for preventing the growth of fascism and its accession to power.

Fascism - A ferocious but unstable power

The fascist dictatorship of the bourgeoisie is a ferocious power, but an unstable one.

What are the chief causes of the instability of fascist dictatorship?

Fascism undertakes to overcome the differences and antagonisms within the bourgeois camp, but it makes these antagonisms even more acute.

Fascism tries to establish its political monopoly by violently destroying other political parties. But the existence of the capitalist system, the existence of various classes and the accentuation of class contradictions inevitably tend to undermine and explode the political monopoly of fascism. In a fascist country the party of the fascists cannot set itself the aim of abolishing classes and class contradictions. It puts an end to the legal existence of bourgeois parties. But a number of them continue to maintain an illegal existence, while the Communist Party even in conditions of illegality continues to make progress, becomes steeled and tempered and leads the struggle of the proletariat against the fascist dictatorship. Hence, under the blows of class contradictions, the political monopoly of fascism is bound to explode.

Another reason for the instability of the fascist dictatorship is that the contrast between the anti-capitalist demagogy of fascism and its policy of enriching the monopolist bourgeoisie in the most piratical fashion makes it easier to expose the class nature of fascism and tends to shake and narrow its mass basis.

Furthermore, the victory of fascism arouses the deep hatred and indignation of the masses, helps to revolutionize them, and provides a powerful stimulus for a united front of the proletariat against fascism.

By conducting a policy of economic nationalism (autarchy) and by seizing the greater part of the national income for the purpose of preparing for war, fascism undermines the whole economic life of the country and accentuates the economic war between the capitalist states. To the conflicts that arise among the bourgeoisie it lends the character of sharp and at times bloody collisions that undermine the stability of the fascist state power in the eyes of the people. A government which murders its own followers, as happened in Germany on June 30 [8] of last year, a fascist government against which another section of the fascist bourgeoisie is conducting an armed fight (the National-Socialist *putsch* in Austria and the violent attacks of individual fascist groups on the fascist government in Poland, Bulgaria, Finland and other countries) -- a government of this character cannot for long maintain its authority in the eyes of the broad mass of the petty bourgeoisie.

The working class must be able to take advantage of the antagonisms and conflicts within the bourgeois camp, but it must not cherish the illusion that fascism will exhaust itself of its own accord. Fascism will not collapse automatically. Only the revolutionary activity of the working class can help to take advantage of the conflicts which inevitably arise within the bourgeois camp in order to undermine the fascist dictatorship and to overthrow it.

By destroying the relics of bourgeois democracy, by elevating open violence to a system of government, fascism shakes democratic illusions and undermines the authority of the law in the eyes of the working people. This is particularly true in countries such as Austria and Spain, where the workers have

32

taken up arms against fascism. In Austria, the heroic struggle of the Schutzbund and the Communists in spite of its defeat, shook the stability of the fascist dictatorship from the very outset.

In Spain, the bourgeoisie did not succeed in putting the fascist muzzle on the working people. The armed struggles in Austria and Spain have resulted in ever wider masses of the working class coming to realize the necessity for a revolutionary class struggle.

Only such monstrous philistines, such lackeys of the bourgeoisie, as the superannuated theoretician of the Second International, Karl Kautsky, are capable of casting reproaches at the workers, to the effect that they should not have taken up arms in Austria and Spain. What would the working class movement in Austria and Spain look like today if the working class of these countries were guided by the treacherous counsels of the Kautskys? The working class would be experiencing profound demoralization in its ranks.

The school of civil war -- Lenin says -- does not leave the people unaffected. It is a harsh school, and its complete curriculum *inevitably* includes the victories of the counterrevolution, the debaucheries of enraged reactionaries, savage punishments meted out by the old governments to the rebels, etc. But only downright pedants and mentally decrepit mummies can grieve over the fact that nations are entering this painful school; this school teaches the oppressed classes how to conduct civil war; it teaches how to bring about a victorious revolution; it concentrates in the masses of present-day slaves that hatred which is always harboured by the downtrodden, dull, ignorant slaves, and which leads those slaves who have become conscious of the shame of their slavery to the greatest historic exploits.
[V. I. Lenin, Collected Works 15:183]

The triumph of fascism in Germany has, as we know, been followed by a new wave of the fascist offensive, which in

Austria led to the provocation by Dollfuss, in Spain to the new onslaughts of counter-revolution on the revolutionary conquests of the masses, in Poland to the fascist reform of the constitution, while in France it spurred the armed detachments of the fascists to attempt a coup d'état in February 1934. But this victory, and the frenzy of the fascist dictatorship, called forth a countermovement for a united proletarian front against fascism on an international scale.

The burning of the Reichstag, which served as a signal for the general attack of fascism on the working class, the seizure and spoliation of the trade unions and the other working class organizations, the groans of the tortured anti-fascists rising from the vaults of the fascist barracks and concentration camps, are making clear to the masses what has been the outcome of the reactionary, disruptive role played by the German Social-Democratic leaders, who rejected the proposal made by the Communists for a joint struggle against advancing fascism. These things are convincing the masses of the necessity of uniting all forces of the working class for the overthrow of fascism.

Hitler's victory also provided a decisive stimulus for the creation of a united front of the working class against fascism in France. Hitler's victory not only aroused in the workers a fear of the fate that befell the German workers, not only kindled hatred for the executioners of their German class brothers, but also strengthened in them the determination never in any circumstances to allow in their country what happened to the working class in Germany.

The powerful urge towards a united front in all the capitalist countries shows that the lessons of defeat have not been in vain. The working class is beginning to act in a *new way*. The initiative shown by the Communist Parties in the organization of a united front and the supreme self-sacrifice displayed by the Communists, by the revolutionary workers in the struggle against fascism, have resulted in an unprecedented increase in the prestige of the Communist International. At the same time, the Second International is undergoing a profound crisis, a crisis which is particularly noticeable and has particularly accentuated since the bankruptcy of German Social-Democracy. With ever greater ease the Social-Democratic workers are able to convince themselves that fascist Germany, with all its horrors and barbarities, is in the final analysis *the result of the Social-Democratic policy of class collaboration* with the bourgeoisie. These masses are coming ever more clearly to realize that the path along which the German Social-Democratic leaders led the proletariat must not be traversed again. Never has there been such ideological dissension in the camp of the Second International as at the present time. A process of differentiation is taking place in all Social-Democratic Parties. Within their ranks *two principal camps* are forming: side by side with the existing camp of reactionary elements, who are trying in every way to preserve the bloc between the Social-Democrats and the bourgeoisie, and who rabidly reject a united front with the Communists, *there is beginning to emerge a camp of revolutionary elements who entertain doubts as to the correctness of the policy of class collaboration with the bourgeoisie, who are in favor of the creation of a united front with the Communists, and who are increasingly coming to adopt the position of the revolutionary class struggle.*

Thus fascism, which appeared as the result of the decline of the capitalist system, in the long run acts as a factor in its *further disintegration.* Thus fascism, which has undertaken to bury Marxism, the revolutionary movement of the working class, is, as a result of the dialectics of life and the class struggle, itself leading to the further *development of the forces* that are bound to serve as its grave-diggers, the grave-diggers of capitalism.

•

II. UNITED FRONT OF THE WORKING CLASS AGAINST FASCISM

Comrades, millions of workers and working people of the capitalist countries are asking the question: How can fascism be prevented from coming to power and how can fascism be overthrown after it has attained power? To this the Communist International replies: *The first thing that must be done, the thing with which to begin, is to form a united front, to establish unity of action of the workers in every factory, in every district, in every region, in every country, all over the world. Unity of action of the proletariat on a national and international scale is the mighty weapon which renders the working class capable not only of successful defense but also of successful counterattack against fascism, against the class enemy.*

Significance of the United Front

Is it not clear that joint action by the supporters of the parties and organizations of the two Internationals, the Communist and the Second International, would make it easier for the masses to repulse the fascist onslaught, and would heighten the political importance of the working class?

Joint action by the parties of both internationals against fascism, however, would not be confined in its effects to influencing their present adherents, the Communists and Social-Democrats; it would also exert a powerful impact on the ranks of the *Catholic, Anarchist and unorganized workers, even upon those who have temporarily become the victims of fascist demagogy.*

Moreover, a powerful united front of the proletariat would exert tremendous influence on *all other strata of the working people*, on the peasantry, on the urban petty bourgeoisie, on the intelligentsia. A united front would inspire the wavering groups with faith in the strength of the working class.

But even this is not all. The proletariat of the imperialist countries has possible allies not only in the working people of its own countries, but also in the *oppressed nations of the colonies and semi-colonies.* Inasmuch as the proletariat is split both nationally and internationally, inasmuch as one of its parts supports the policy of collaboration with the bourgeoisie, in particular its system of oppression in the colonies and semi-colonies, a barrier is put between the working class and the oppressed peoples of the colonies and semi-colonies, and the world anti-imperialist front is weakened. Every step by the proletariat of the imperialist countries on the road to unity of action in the direction of supporting the struggle for the liberation of the colonial peoples means transforming the colonies and semi-colonies into one of the most important reserves of the world proletariat.

If, finally, we bear in mind that international unity of action by the proletariat relies on the steadily growing strength of the proletarian state, the land of socialism, the Soviet Union, we see what broad perspectives are revealed by the realization of proletarian unity of action on a national and international scale.

The establishment of unity of action by all sections of the working class, irrespective of the party or organization to which they belong, is necessary *even before the majority of the working class is united in the struggle for the overthrow of capitalism and the victory of the proletarian revolution.*

Is it possible to realize this unity of action of the proletariat in the individual countries and throughout the whole world? Yes, it is. And it is possible at this very moment. The Communist International *puts no conditions for unity of action except one, and at that an elementary condition acceptable to all workers, viz., that the unity of action be directed against fascism, against the offensive of capital, against the threat of war, against the class enemy.* This is our condition.

The chief arguments of the opponents of the United Front

What objections can the opponents of the united front have, and what objections do they voice?

Some say: **"The Communists use the slogan of the united front merely as a maneuver."** But if this is the case, we reply, why don't you expose this "Communist maneuver" by your honest participation in the united front? We declare frankly: We want unity of action by the working class so that the proletariat may grow strong in its struggle against the bourgeoisie, in order that while defending today its current interests against attacking capital, against fascism, the proletariat may reach a position tomorrow to create the preliminary conditions for its final emancipation.

"The Communists attack us," say others. But listen, we have repeatedly declared: We shall not attack anyone, whether persons, organizations or parties, standing for the united front of the working class against the class enemy. But at the same time it is our duty, in the interests of the proletariat and its cause, to criticize those persons, organizations and parties that hinder unity of action by the workers.

"We cannot form a united front with the Communists, since they have a different program," says a third group. But you yourselves say that your program differs from the program of the bourgeois parties, and yet this did not and does not prevent you from entering into coalitions with these parties.

"The bourgeois-democratic parties are better allies against fascism that the Communists," say the opponents of the united front and the advocates of coalition with the bourgeoisie. But what does Germany's experience teach? Did not the Social-Democrats form a bloc with those "better" allies? And what were the results?

"If we establish a united front with the Communists, the petty bourgeoisie will take fright at the 'Red danger' and will desert to the fascists," we hear it said quite frequently. But does the united front represent a threat to the peasants, small traders, artisans, working intellectuals? No, the united front is a threat to the big bourgeoisie, the financial magnates, the junkers and other exploiters, whose regime brings complete ruin to all these strata.

"Social-Democracy is for democracy, the Communists are for dictatorship; therefore we cannot form a united front with the Communists," say some of the Social-Democratic leaders. But are we offering you now a united front for the purpose of proclaiming the dictatorship of the proletariat? We make no such proposal now.

"Let the Communists recognize democracy, let them come out in its defense; then we shall be ready for a united front." To this we reply: We are the adherents of Soviet democracy, the democracy of the working people, the most consistent democracy in the world. But in the capitalist countries we defend and shall continue to defend every inch of bourgeois-democratic liberties, which are being attacked by fascism and bourgeois reaction, because the interests of the class struggle of the proletariat so dictate.

"But can the tiny Communist Parties contribute anything by participating in the united front brought about by the Labour Party," say, for instance, the Labour leaders of Great Britain. Remember how the Austrian Social-Democratic leaders said the same thing with reference to the small Austrian Communist Party. And what have events shown? It was not the Austrian Social-Democratic Party headed by Otto Bauer and

42

Renner that proved right, but the small Austrian Communist Party which signalled the fascist danger in Austria at the right moment and called upon the workers to struggle. The whole experience of the labor movement has shown that the Communists with all their relative insignificance in numbers, are the motive power of the militant activity of the proletariat. Moreover, it must not be forgotten that the Communist Parties of Austria or Great Britain are not only the tens of thousands of workers who are adherents of the Party, but are parts of the world Communist movement, are Sections of the Communist International, whose leading Party is the Party of a proletariat which has already achieved victory and rules over one-sixth of the globe.

"But the united front did not prevent fascism from being victorious in the Saar," is another objection advanced by the opponents of the united front. Strange is the logic of these gentlemen. First they leave no stone unturned to ensure the victory of fascism and then they rejoice with malicious glee because the united front which they entered into only at the last moment did not lead to the victory of the workers.

"If we were to form a united front with the Communists, we should have to withdraw from the coalition, and reactionary and fascist parties would enter the government," say the Social-Democratic leaders holding cabinet posts in various countries. Very well. Was not the German Social-Democratic Party in a coalition government? It was. Was not the Austrian Social-Democratic Party in office? Were not the Spanish Socialists in the same government as the bourgeoisie? They were. Did the participation of the Social-Democratic Parties in the bourgeois coalition governments in these countries prevent fascism from attacking the proletariat? It did not. Consequently it is as clear as daylight that participation of Social-Democratic ministers in bourgeois governments is *not* a barrier to fascism.

43

"The Communists act like dictators, they want to prescribe and dictate everything to us." No. We prescribe nothing and dictate nothing. We only put forward our proposals, being convinced that if realized they will meet the interests of the working people. This is not only the right but the duty of all those acting in the name of the workers. You are afraid of the 'dictatorship' of the Cornmunists? Let us jointly submit to the workers all proposals, both yours and ours, jointly discuss them together with all the workers, and choose those proposals which are most useful to the cause of the working class.

Thus all these arguments against a united front *will not stand the slightest criticism.* They are rather the flimsy excuses of the reactionary leaders of Social-Democracy, who prefer their united front with the bourgeoisie to the united front of the proletariat.

No. These excuses will not hold water. The international proletariat has experienced the suffering caused by the split in the working class, and becomes more and more convinced that *the united front, the unity of action of the proletariat on a national and international scale, is at once necessary and perfectly possible.*

Content and forms of the united front

What is and ought to be the basic content of the united front at the present stage? The defense of the immediate economic and political interests of the working class, the defense of the working class against fascism, must form the *starting point* and *main content* of the united front in all capitalist countries.

We must not confine ourselves to bare appeals to struggle for the proletarian dictatorship. We must find and advance those slogans and forms of struggle which arise from the vital needs of the masses, from the level of their fighting capacity at the present stage of development.

We must point out to the masses what they must do *today* to defend themselves against capitalist spoliation and fascist barbarity.

We must strive to establish the widest united front with the aid of joint action by workers' organizations of different trends for the defense of the vital interests of the laboring masses. This means:

- *First*, joint struggle really to shift the burden of the consequences of the crisis onto the shoulders of the ruling classes, the shoulders of the capitalists and landlords -- in a word, onto the shoulders of the rich.
- *Second*, joint struggle against all forms of the fascist offensive, in defense of the gains and the rights of the working people, against the abolition of bourgeois-democratic liberties.
- *Third*, joint struggle against the approaching danger of an imperialist war, a struggle that will make

the preparation of such a war more difficult.

We must tirelessly prepare the working class for a *rapid change in forms and methods of struggle* when there is a change in the situation. As the movement grows and the unity of the working class strengthens, we must go further, and prepare the transition *from the defensive to the offensive against capital*, steering towards the *organization of a mass political strike*. It must be an absolute condition of such a strike to draw into it the main trade unions of the countries concerned.

Communists, of course, cannot and must not for a moment abandon their own *independent work* of Communist education, organization and mobilization of the masses. However, to ensure that the workers find the road of unity of action, it is necessary to strive at the same time both for short-term and for long-term agreements that provide for *joint action with Social Democratic Parties, reformist trade unions and other organizations of the working people* against the class enemies of the proletariat. The chief stress in all this must be laid on developing *mass action*, locally, *to be carried out by the local organizations* through local agreements. While loyally carrying out the conditions of all agreements made with them, we shall mercilessly expose all sabotage of joint action on the part of persons and organizations participating in the united front. To any attempt to wreck the agreements -- and such attempts may possibly be made -- we shall reply by appealing to the masses while continuing untiringly to struggle for restoration of the broken unity of action.

It goes without saying that the practical realization of a united front will take *various* forms in various countries, depending upon the condition and character of the workers' organizations and their political level, upon the situation in the particular country, upon the changes in progress in the international labor movement, etc.

These forms may include, for instance: coordinated joint

action of the workers to be agreed upon *from case to case* on definite occasions, on individual demands or on the basis of a common platform; coordinated actions in *individual enterprises or by whole industries;* coordinated actions on a *local, regional, national* or *international scale,* coordinated actions for the organization of the *economic* struggle of the workers, for carrying out mass *political* actions, for the organization of joint *self-defense* against fascist attacks, coordinated actions in rendering *aid to political prisoners and their families,* in the field of struggle against *social reaction;* joint actions in the defense of the *interests of the youth and women,* in the field of the *cooperative movement, cultural activity, sport,* etc.

It would be insufficient to rest content with the conclusion of a pact providing for joint action and the formation of contact committees from the parties and organizations participating in the united front, like those we have in France, for instance. That is only the first step. The pact is an auxiliary means for obtaining joint action, but by itself it does not constitute a united front. A contact commission between the leaders of the Communist and Socialist Parties is necessary to facilitate the carrying out of joint action, but by itself it is far from adequate for a real development of the united front, for drawing the widest masses into the struggle against fascism.

The Communists and all revolutionary workers must strive for the formation of elected (and in the countries of fascist dictatorship -- selected from among the most authoritative participants in the united front movement) *nonparty class bodies of the united front,* at the *factories,* among the *unemployed,* in the *working class districts,* among the small *towns-folk* and in the *villages.* Only such bodies will be able to include also the vast masses of unorganized working people in the united front movement, and will be able to assist in developing mass initiative in the struggle against the capitalist offensive, against fascism and reaction, and on this basis create the necessary *broad active rank-and-file of the united front* and train hundreds and thousands of non-Party Bolsheviks in the capitalist countries.

Joint action of the *organized* workers is the beginning, the foundation. But we must not lose sight of the fact that the unorganized masses constitute the vast majority of workers. Thus, in *France* the number of organized workers -- Communists, Socialists, trade union members of various trends-is altogether *about one million*, while the total number of workers is eleven million. In *Great Britain* there are approximately *five million* members of trade unions and parties of various trends. At the same time the total number of workers is *fourteen million.* In the *United States of America* about *five million* workers are organized, while altogether there are *thirty-eight million* workers in that country. About the same ratio holds good for a number of other countries. In "normal" times this mass in the main does not participate in political life. But now this gigantic mass is getting into motion more and more, is being brought into political life, comes out onto the political arena.

The creation of nonpartisan class bodies is the *best form* for carrying out, extending and strengthening a united front among the rank-and-file of the masses. These bodies will likewise be the best bulwark against any attempt of the opponents of the united front to disrupt the growing unity of action of the working class.

The anti-fascist people's front

In mobilizing the mass of working people for the struggle against fascism, the formation of a *wide anti-fascist People's Front* on the basis of the *proletarian united front* is a particularly important task. The success of the whole struggle of the proletariat is closely bound up with the establishment of a fighting alliance between the proletariat, on the one hand, and the laboring peasantry and basic mass of the urban petty bourgeoisie who together form the majority of the population even in industrially developed countries, on the other.

In its agitation, fascism, desirous of winning these masses to its own side, tries to set the mass of the working people in town and countryside against the revolutionary proletariat, frightening the petty bourgeoisie with the bogey of the "Red peril." We must *turn this weapon against those who wield it* and show the working peasants, artisans and intellectuals whence the real danger threatens. We must show concretely who it is that piles the burden of taxes and imposts onto the peasant and squeezes usurious interest out of him; who it is that, while owning the best land and every form of wealth, drives the peasant and his family from their plot of land and dooms them to unemployment and poverty. We must explain concretely, patiently and persistently who it is that ruins the artisans and handicraftsmen with taxes, imposts, high rents and competition impossible for them to withstand; who it is that throws into the street and deprives of employment the wide masses of the working intelligentsia.

But this is *not enough*.

The fundamental, the most decisive thing in establishing

an anti-fascist People's Front is *resolute action of the revolutionary proletariat* in defense of the demands of these sections of the people, particularly the working peasantry -- demands in line with the basic interests of the proletariat -- and in the process of struggle combining the demands of the working class with these demands.

In forming an anti-fascist People's Front, a correct approach to those organizations and parties whose membership comprises a considerable number of the working peasantry and the mass of the urban petty bourgeoisie is of great importance.

In the capitalist countries the majority of these parties and organizations, political as well as economic, are still under the influence of the bourgeoisie and follow it. The social composition of these parties and organizations is heterogeneous. They include rich peasants side by side with landless peasants, big businessmen alongside petty shopkeepers; but control is in the hands of the former, the agents of big capital. This obliges us to *approach the different organizations in different ways*, remembering that often the bulk of the membership ignores the real political character of its leadership. Under certain conditions we can and must try to draw these parties and organizations or certain sections of them to the side of the anti-fascist People's Front, despite their bourgeois leadership. Such, for instance, is today the situation in France with the Radical party, in the United States with various farmers' organizations, in Poland with the "Stronnictwo Ludowe," 9) in Yugoslavia with the Croatian Peasants' Party, in Bulgaria with the Agrarian Union, in Greece with the Agrarians, etc. But regardless of whether or not there is any chance of attracting these parties and organizations as a whole to the People's Front, our tactics must *under all circumstances* be directed towards drawing the small peasants, artisans, handicraftsmen, etc., among their members into an anti-fascist People's Front.

Hence, you see that in this field we must all along the

line put an end to what has not infrequently occurred in our work-neglect or contempt of the various organizations and parties of the peasants, artisans and the mass of petty bourgeoisie in the towns.

Key questions of the United Front in individual countries

In every country there are certain *key questions*, which at the present stage are agitating vast masses of the population and around which the struggle for the establishment of a united front must be developed. If these key points, or key questions, are properly grasped it will ensure and accelerate the establishment of a united front.

The United States of America

Let us take, for example, so important a country in the capitalist world as *the United States of America*. There millions of people have been set into motion by the crisis. The program for the recovery of capitalism has collapsed. Vast masses are beginning to abandon the bourgeois parties and are at present at the crossroads.

Embryo American fascism is trying to direct the disillusionment and discontent of these masses into reactionary fascist channels. It is a peculiarity of the development of American fascism that at the present stage it comes forward principally in the guise of an opposition to fascism, which it accuses of being an "un-American" trend imported from abroad. In contradistinction to German fascism, which acts under anti-constitutional slogans, American fascism tries to portray itself as the custodian of the Constitution and "American democracy." It does not as yet represent a directly menacing force. But if it succeeds in penetrating the wide masses who have become disillusioned with the old bourgeois parties, it may become a serious menace in the very near future.

And what would the victory of fascism in the United States involve? For the mass of working people it would of course, involve the unprecedented strengthening of the regime of exploitation and the destruction of the working-class movement. And what would be the international significance of this victory of fascism? As we known, the United States is not Hungary, nor Finland, nor Bulgaria, nor Latvia. The victory of fascism in the United States would vitally change the whole international situation.

Under these circumstances, can the American proletariat content itself with organizing only its class conscious vanguard, which is prepared to follow the revolutionary path? No.

It is perfectly obvious that the interests of the American proletariat demand that all its forces dissociate themselves from the capitalist parties without delay. It must find in good time ways and suitable forms to prevent fascism from winning over the wide mass of discontented working people. And here it must be said that under American conditions the creation of a mass party of the working people, a *Workers' and Farmers' Party*, might serve as such a suitable form. *Such a party would be a specific form of the mass People's Front in America* and should be put in opposition to the parties of the trusts and the banks, and likewise to growing fascism. Such a party, of course, will be *neither* Socialist *nor* Communist. But it *must be* an anti-fascist party and *must not be* an anti-Communist party. The program of this party must be directed against the banks, trusts and monopolies, against the principal enemies of the people, who are gambling on the woes of the latter. Such a party will justify its name only if it defends the urgent demands of the working class; only if it fights for genuine social legislation, for unemployment insurance; only if it fights for land for the white and Black sharecroppers and for their liberation from debt burdens; only if it tries to secure the cancellation of the farmers'

54

indebtedness; only if it fights for an equal status for Negroes; only if it defends the demands of the war veterans and the interests of members of the liberal professions, small businessmen and artisans. And so on.

It goes without saying that such a party will fight for the election of its own candidates to local government, to the state legislatures, to the House of Representatives and the Senate.

Our comrades in the United States acted rightly in taking the initiative in the setting up of such a party. But they still have to take effective measures in order to make the creation of such a party the cause of the masses themselves. The questions of forming a Workers' and Farmers' Party, and its program should be discussed at mass meetings of the people. We should develop the most widespread movement for the creation of such a party, and take the lead in it. In no case must the initiative of organizing the party be allowed to pass to elements desirous of utilizing the discontent of the millions who have become disillusioned in both the bourgeois parties, Democratic and Republican, in order to create a "third party" in the United States as an anti-Communist party, a party directed against the revolutionary movement.

Great Britain

In *Great Britain*, as a result of the mass action of the British workers, Mosley's fascist organization has for the time being been pushed into the background. But we must not close our eyes to the fact that the so-called "National Government" is passing a number of reactionary measures directed against the working class, as a result of which conditions are being created in Great Britain, too, which will make it easier for the bourgeoisie, if necessary, to pass to a fascist regime.

At the present stage, fighting the fascist danger in Great Britain means primarily fighting the "National Government" and its reactionary measures, fighting the offensive of capital, fighting for the demands of the unemployed, fighting against wage cuts and for the repeal of all those laws with the help of which the British bourgeoisie is lowering the standard of living of the masses.

But the growing hatred of the working class for the "National Government" is uniting increasingly large numbers under the slogan of the formation of a *new Labor Government* in Great Britain. Can the Communists ignore this frame of mind of the masses, who still retain faith in a Labor Government? No, Comrades. We must find a way of approaching these masses. We tell them openly, as did the Thirteenth Congress of the British Communist Party, that we Communists are in favor of a soviet government *["soviet" meant a workers' and peasants' council, or people's council, in a system that nationalized the major resources and means of production]* as the only form of government capable of emancipating the workers from the yoke of the capital. But you want a Labor Government? Very well. We have been and are fighting hand in hand with you for the defeat of the "National Government." We are prepared to support your fight for the formation of a new Labor government, in spite of the fact that both the previous Labor governments failed to fulfil the promises made to the working class by the Labour Party. We do not expect this government to carry out socialist measures. But *we shall present it with the demand*, in the name of millions of workers, that it defend the most essential economic and political interests of the working class and of all working people. Let us jointly discuss a common program of such demands, and let us achieve that unity of action which the proletariat requires in order to repel the reactionary offensive of the "National Government," the attack of capital and fascism and the preparations for a new war. On this basis, the British comrades are prepared at the forthcoming parliamentary elections to cooperate with branches of the Labour Party against the "National Government," and also against Lloyd George who is trying in his own way in the interests of the British bourgeoisie to lure the masses into following him against the cause of the working class.

The position of the British Communists is a correct one. It will help them to set up a militant united front with the millions of members of the British trade unions and Labour Party. While always remaining in the front ranks of the fighting proletariat, and pointing out to the masses the only right path -- the path of struggle for the revolutionary overthrow of the rule of the bourgeoisie and the establishment of a soviet government -- the Communists, in defining their immediate political aims, must not attempt to leap over those necessary stages of the mass movement in the course of which the working class by its own experience outlives its illusions and passes over to Communism.

France

France, as we know, is a country in which the working class is setting an example to the whole international proletariat of how to fight fascism. The French Communist Party is setting an example to all the sections of the Comintern of how the tactics of the united front should be applied; the Socialist workers are setting an example of what the Social-Democratic workers of other capitalist countries should now be doing in the fight against fascism.

The significance of the anti-fascist demonstration attended by half a million people in Paris on July 14 of this year, and of the numerous demonstrations in other French cities, is tremendous.

This is not merely a United Front movement of the workers; it is the beginning of a wide general front of the people against fascism in France. This united front movement enhances the confidence of the working class in its own forces; it strengthens its consciousness of the leading role it is playing in relation to the peasantry, the urban petty bourgeoisie, and the intelligentsia; it extends the influence of the Communist Party among the mass of the working class and therefore makes the proletariat stronger in the fight against fascism. It is arousing in good time the vigilance of the masses in regard to the fascist danger. And it will serve as a contagious example for the development of the anti-fascist struggle in other capitalist countries, and will exercise a heartening influence on the proletarians of Germany, oppressed by the fascist dictatorship.

The victory, needless to say, is a big one; but still it does not decide the issue of the anti-fascist struggle. The overwhelming majority of the French people are undoubtedly opposed to fascism. But the bourgeoisie is able by armed force to violate the popular will. The fascist movement is continuing to develop absolutely freely, with the active support of monopoly capital, the state apparatus of the bourgeoisie, the general staff of the French army, and the reactionary leaders of the Catholic Church -- that stronghold of all reaction. The most powerful fascist organization, the *Croix de Feu*, now commands 300,000 armed men, the backbone of which consists of 60,000 officers of the reserve. It holds strong positions in the police, the gendarmerie, the army, the air force and in all government offices. The recent municipal elections have shown that in France it is not only the revolutionary forces that are growing, but also the forces of fascism. If fascism succeeds in penetrating widely among the peasantry and in securing the support of one section of the army, while the other section remains neutral, the masses of the French working people will not be able to prevent the fascists from coming to power. Comrades, do not forget the organizational weakness of the French labor movement which facilitates a fascist offensive. The working class and all anti-fascists in France have no grounds for resting content with the results achieved so far.

What are the tasks facing the working class in France?

First, to establish a united front not only in the political sphere, but also in the economic sphere, in order to organize the struggle against the capitalist offensive, and by its pressure to smash the resistance offered to the united front by the leaders of the reformist Confederation of Labor.

Second, to achieve trade union unity in France -- united trade unions based on the class struggle.

Third, to enlist the broad mass of the peasants and petty bourgeoisie in the anti-fascist movement, devoting special attention to their urgent demands in the program of the anti-fascist People's Front.

Fourth, to strengthen organizationally and extend further the anti-fascist movement which has already developed, by the widespread creation of nonpartisan elected bodies of the anti-fascist People's Front, whose influence will extend to wider masses than those in the present parties and organizations of the working people in France.

Fifth, to force the disbanding and disarming of the fascist organizations, as being organizations of conspirators against the republic and agents of Hitler in France.

Sixth, to secure that the state apparatus, army and police shall be purged of the conspirators who are preparing a fascist coup.

Seventh, to develop the struggle against the leaders of the reactionary cliques of the Catholic Church, one of the most important strongholds of French fascism.

Eighth, to link up the army with the anti-fascist movement by creating in its ranks committees for the defense of the republic and the constitution, directed against those who want to utilize the army for an anti-constitutional coup d'état; to prevent the reactionary forces in France from wrecking the Franco-Soviet pact, which defends the cause of peace against the aggression of German fascism.

And if in France the anti-fascist movement leads to the formation of a government which will carry on a real struggle against French fascism -- not in words but in deeds -- and which will carry out the program of demands of the antifascist People's Front, the Communists, while remaining the irreconcilable foes of every bourgeois government and supporters of a soviet government, will nevertheless, in face of the growing fascist danger, be prepared to support such a government.

The United Front and the fascist mass organizations

Comrades, the fight for the establishment of a united front in countries where the fascists are in power is perhaps the most important problem facing us. In such countries, of course, the fight is carried on under far more difficult conditions than in countries with a legal labor movement. Nevertheless, all the conditions exist in fascist countries for the development of a real anti-fascist People's Front in the struggle against the fascist dictatorship since the Social-Democratic, Catholic and other workers, in Germany for instance, are able to realize more directly the need for a joint struggle with the Communists against the fascist dictatorship. Wide strata of the petty bourgeoisie and the peasantry, having already tasted the bitter fruits of fascist rule, are growing increasingly discontented and disillusioned which makes it easier to enlist them in the antifascist People's Front.

The principal task in fascist countries, particularly in Germany and Italy, where fascism has managed to gain a mass basis and has forced the workers and other working people into its organizations, consists in skilfully combining the fight against the fascist dictatorship from without with the undermining of it from within, inside the fascist mass organizations and bodies. Special methods and means of approach, suited to the concrete conditions prevailing in these countries, must be learned, mastered and applied, so as to facilitate the rapid disintegration of the mass base of fascism and to prepare the way for the overthrow of the fascist dictatorship. We must learn, master and apply this, and not only shout "Down with Hitler" and "Down with Mussolini." Yes, learn, master and apply.

This is a difficult and complex task. It is all the more difficult in that our experience in successfully combating a fascist dictatorship is extremely limited. Our Italian comrades, for instance, have already been fighting under the conditions of a fascist dictatorship for about thirteen --years. Nevertheless, they have not yet succeeded in developing a real mass struggle against fascism, and therefore they have unfortunately been little able in this respect to help the Communist Parties in other fascist countries by their positive experience.

The Germany and Italian Communists, and the Communists in other fascist countries, as well as the Communist youth, have displayed prodigious valor; they have made and are daily making tremendous sacrifices. We all bow our heads in honor of such heroism and sacrifices. But heroism alone is not enough. Heroism must be combined with day-to-day work among the masses, with concrete struggle against fascism, so as to achieve the most tangible results in this sphere. In our struggle against fascist dictatorship it is particularly dangerous to confuse the wish with fact. We must base ourselves on the facts, on the actual concrete situation.

What is now the actual situation in Germany, for instance?

The masses are becoming increasingly restless and disillusioned with the policy of the fascist dictatorship, and this even assumes the form of partial strikes and other actions. In spite of all its efforts, fascism has failed to win over politically the basic masses of the workers; it is losing even its former supporters, and will lose them more and more in the future. Nevertheless, we must realize that the workers who are convinced of the possibility of overthrowing the fascist dictatorship, and who are already prepared to fight for it actively, are still in the minority -- they consist of us, the Communists, and the revolutionary section of the Social-

Democratic workers. But the majority of the working people have not yet become aware of the real, concrete possibilities and methods of overthrowing this dictatorship, and still adopt a waiting attitude. This we must bear in mind when we outline our tasks in the struggle against fascism in Germany, and when we seek, study and apply special methods of approach for the undermining and overthrow of the fascist dictatorship in Germany.

In order to be able to strike a telling blow at the fascist dictatorship, we must first find out what is its most vulnerable point. What is the Achilles' heel of the fascist dictatorship? Its social basis. The latter is extremely heterogeneous. It is made up of various strata of society. Fascism has proclaimed itself the sole representative of all classes and strata of the population: the manufacturer and the worker, the millionaire and the unemployed, the Junker and the small peasant, the big businessman and the artisan. It pretends to defend the interests of all these strata, the interests of the nation. But since it is a dictatorship of the big bourgeoisie, fascism must inevitably come into conflict with its mass social basis, all the more since, under the fascist dictatorship, the class contradictions between the pack of financial magnates and the overwhelming majority of the people are brought out in greatest relief.

We can lead the masses to a decisive struggle for the overthrow of the fascist dictatorship only by getting the workers who have been forced into the fascist organizations, or have joined them through ignorance, to take part in the most elementary movements for the defense of their economic, political and cultural interests. It is for this reason that the Communists must work in these organizations, as the best champions of the day-to-day interests of the mass of members, bearing in mind that as the workers belonging to these organizations begin more and more frequently to demand their rights and defend their interests, they inevitably come into conflict with the fascist dictatorship.

In defending the urgent and at first the most elementary interests of the working people in town and countryside it is comparatively easier to find a common language not only with the conscious anti-fascists, but also with those of the working people who are still supporters of fascism, but are disillusioned and dissatisfied with its policy and are grumbling and seeking an occasion for expressing their discontent. In general, we must realize that all our tactics in countries with a fascist dictatorship must be of such a character as not to repulse the rank-and-file followers of fascism drawn from the working sections of society.

We need not be dismayed, comrades, if the people mobilized around these day-to-day interests consider themselves either indifferent to politics or even followers of fascism. The important thing for us is to draw them into the movement, which, although it may not at first proceed openly under the slogans of the struggle against fascism, is already objectively an anti-fascist movement putting these masses into opposition to the fascist dictatorship.

Experience teaches us that the view that it is generally impossible, in countries with a fascist dictatorship, to come out legally or semi-legally, is harmful and incorrect. To insist on this point of view means to fall into passivity, and to renounce real mass work altogether. True, under the conditions of a fascist dictatorship, to find forms and methods of legal or semi-legal action is a difficult and complex problem. But, as in many other questions, the path is indicated by life itself and by the initiative of the masses themselves, who have already provided us with a number of examples that must be generalized and applied in an organized and effective manner.

We must very resolutely put an end to the tendency to underestimate work in the fascist mass organizations. In Italy, in Germany and in a number of other fascist countries, our comrades tried to conceal their passivity, and frequently even their direct refusal to work in the fascist mass organizations, by putting forward work in the factories as against work in the fascist mass organizations. In reality however, it was just this mechanical distinction which led to work being conducted very feebly, and sometimes not at all, both in the fascist mass organizations and in the factories.

Yet it is particularly important that Communists in the fascist countries should be wherever the masses are to be found. Fascism has deprived the workers of their own legal organizations. It has forced the fascist organizations upon them, and it is *there that the masses are* -- by compulsion, or to some extent voluntarily. These mass fascist organizations can and must be made our legal or semi-legal field of action where we can meet the masses. They can and must be made our legal or semi-legal starting point for the defense of the day-to-day interests of the masses. To utilize these possibilities, Communists must win elected positions in the fascist mass organizations, for contact with the masses, and must rid themselves once and for all of the prejudice that such activity is unseemly and unworthy of a revolutionary worker.

In Germany, for instance, there is a system of so-called "shop stewards." But where is it stated that we must leave the fascists a monopoly in these organizations? Cannot we try to unite the Communist, Social-Democratic, Catholic and other anti-fascist workers in the factories so that when the list of "shop stewards" is voted upon, the known agents of the employers may be struck off and other candidates, enjoying the confidence of the workers, inserted in their stead? Practice has already shown that this is possible.

And does not practice also go to show that it is possible jointly with the Social-Democratic and other discontented workers, to demand that the "shop stewards" really defend the interests of the workers?

Take the "Labor Front" in Germany, or the fascist trade unions in Italy. Is it not possible to demand that the functionaries of the Labor Front be elected, and not appointed, to insist that the leading bodies of the local groups report to meetings of the members of the organizations; to address these demands, following a decision by the group, to the employer, to the "labor trustee," to higher bodies of the Labor Front? This is possible, provided the revolutionary workers actually work within the Labor Front and try to obtain posts in it.

Similar methods of work are possible and essential in other mass fascist organizations also -- in the Hitler Youth Leagues, in the sports organizations, in the *Kraft durch Freude* [10] organizations, in the *Dopo lavoro* [11] in Italy, in the cooperatives and so forth.

Comrades, you recall the ancient legend about the capture of Troy. Troy was inaccessible to the armies attacking her, thanks to her impregnable walls. And the attacking army, after suffering heavy casualties, was unable to achieve victory until with the aid of the famous Trojan horse it managed to penetrate to the very heart of the enemy's Camp.

We revolutionary workers, it appears to me, should not be shy about using the same tactics with regard to our fascist foe, who is defending himself against the people with the help of a living wall of his cutthroats.

He who fails to understand the necessity of using such tactics in the case of fascism, he who regards such an approach as "humiliating," may be a most excellent comrade, but if you will allow me to say so, he is a windbag and not a revolutionary, he will be unable to lead the masses to the overthrow of the fascist dictatorship.

The mass movement for a united front, starting with the defense of the most elementary needs, and changing its forms and watchwords of struggle as the latter extends and grows, is

66

growing up outside and inside the fascist organizations in Germany, Italy, and the other countries in which fascism has a mass basis. It will be the battering ram which will shatter the fortress of the fascist dictatorship that at present seems impregnable to many.

The United Front in countries where the social democrats are in office

The struggle for the establishment of a united front raises another very important problem, the problem of a united front in Countries where Social-Democratic governments, or coalition governments in which Socialists participate, are in power, as, for instance, in Denmark, Norway, Sweden, Czechoslovakia and Belgium.

Our attitude of absolute opposition to Social-Democratic governments, which are governments of compromise with the bourgeoisie, is well known. But this notwithstanding, we do not regard the existence of a *Social-Democratic government* or of a government coalition with bourgeois parties as an *insurmountable* obstacle to establishing a united front with the Social-Democrats on certain issues.

We believe that in such a case, too, a united front in defense of the vital interests of the working people and in the struggle against fascism is quite *possible* and *necessary*. It stands to reason that in countries where representatives of Social-Democratic parties take part in the government the Social-Democratic leadership offers the strongest *resistance* to the proletarian united front. This is quite comprehensible. After all, they want to show the bourgeoisie that they, better and more skilfully than anyone else, can keep the discontented working masses under control and prevent them from falling under the influence of Communism.

The fact, however, that Social-Democratic ministers are opposed to the proletarian united front can by no means justify a situation in which *the Communists do nothing to establish a united front of the proletariat.*

Our comrades in the Scandinavian countries often follow the line of least resistance, *confining themselves to propaganda exposing the Social-Democratic governments.* This is a mistake. In **Denmark**, for example, the Social-Democratic leaders have been in the government for the past ten years, and for ten years, day in and day out, the Communists have been reiterating that it is a bourgeois capitalist government. We have to assume that the Danish workers are acquainted with this propaganda. The fact that a considerable majority nevertheless vote for the Social-Democratic government party only goes to show that the Communists' exposure of the government by means of propaganda is *insufficient.* It does *not* prove, however, that these hundreds of thousands of workers are satisfied with all the government measures of the Social-Democratic ministers. No, they are *not satisfied* with the fact that by its so-called crisis 'agreement' the Social-Democratic government assists *the big capitalists and landlords* and not the workers and poor peasants. They are not satisfied with the decree issued by the government in January 1933, which deprived the workers of the *right to strike.* They are not satisfied with the project of the Social Democratic leadership for a dangerous *anti-democratic electoral reform* (which would considerably reduce the number of deputies). I shall hardly be in error, comrades, if I state that 99 per cent of the Danish workers *do not approve* of these political steps taken by the Social-Democratic leaders and ministers.

Is it not possible for the Communists to call upon the trade unions and Social-Democratic organizations of Denmark to discuss some of these burning issues, to express their opinions on them and come out jointly for a proletarian united front with the object of obtaining the workers' demands? In October of last year, when our Danish comrades appealed to the trade unions to act against the reduction of unemployment relief and for the democratic rights of the trade unions, about 100 local trade union organizations joined the united front.

In *Sweden* a Social-Democratic government is in power for the third time, but the Swedish Communists have for a long time abstained from applying the united front tactics in practice. Why? Was it because they were opposed to the united front? Of course not; they were in principle for a united front, for a united front in general, but they failed to understand in what circumstances, on what questions, in defense of what demands a proletarian united front could be successfully established, where and how to "hook on." A few months before the formation of the Social democratic government, the Social Democratic Party advanced during the elections a platform containing a number of demands which would have been the very thing to include in the platform of the proletarian united front. For example, the slogans *Against custom duties, Against militarization, Put an end to the policy of delay in the question of unemployment insurance, Grant adequate old age pensions, Prohibit organizations like the "Munch" corps* (a fascist organization), *Down with class legislation against the unions demanded by the bourgeois parties.*

Over a million of the working people of Sweden voted in 1932 for these demands advanced by the Social-Democrats, and welcomed in 1933 the formation of a Social-Democratic government in the hope that now these demands would be realized. What could have been more natural in such a situation and what would have been better suited the mass of the workers than an appeal of the Communist Party to all Social-Democratic and trade union organizations to take joint action to secure these demands advanced by the Social-Democratic Party?

If we had succeeded in really mobilizing wide masses and in welding the Social-Democratic and Communist workers' organizations into a united front to secure these demands of the Social-Democrats themselves, there is no doubt that the

71

working class of Sweden would have gained thereby. The Social-Democratic ministers of Sweden, of course, would not have been very happy over it, for in that case the government would have been compelled to meet at least some of these demands. At any rate, what has happened now, when the government instead of abolishing has raised some of the duties, instead of restricting militarism has enlarged the military budget, and instead of rejecting all legislation directed against the trade unions has itself introduced such a bill in Parliament, would not have happened. True, on the last issue the Communist party of Sweden carried through a good mass campaign in the spirit of the proletarian united front, with the result that in the end even the Social-Democratic parliamentary faction felt constrained to vote against the government bill, and for the time being it has been voted down.

The *Norwegian* Communists were right in calling upon the organizations of the Labor Party to organize joint May Day demonstrations and in putting forward a number of demands which in the main coincided with the demands contained in the election platform of the Norwegian Labor Party. Although this step in favor of a united front was poorly prepared and the leadership of the Norwegian Labor Party opposed it, united front demonstrations took place in thirty localities.

Formerly many Communists used to be afraid it would be opportunism on their part if they did not counter every partial demand of the Social-Democrats by demands of their own which were twice as radical. That was a naive mistake. If Social-Democrats, for instance, demanded the dissolution of the fascist organizations, there was no reason why we should add: "and the disbanding of the state police" (a demand which would be expedient under different circumstances). We should rather tell the Social-Democratic workers: We are ready to accept these demands of your Party as demands of the proletarian united front and are ready to fight to the end for their realization. Let us join hands for the battle.

In *Czechoslovakia* also certain demands advanced by the Czech and German Social-Democrats, and by the reformist trade unions, can and should be utilized for establishing a united front of the working class. When the Social-Democrats, for instance, demand work for the unemployed or the abolition of the laws restricting municipal self-government, as they have done ever since 1927, these demands should be made concrete in each locality, in each district, and a fight should be carried on hand in hand with the Social-Democratic organizations for their actual realization. Or, when the Social-Democratic Parties thunder "in general terms" against the agents of fascism in the state apparatus, the proper thing to do is in each particular district to drag into the light of day *the particular* local fascist spokesmen, and together with the Social Democratic workers demand their removal from government employ.

In *Belgium* the leaders of the Social-Democratic Party, with Emile Vandervelde at their head, have entered a coalition government. This "success" they achieved thanks to their lengthy and extensive campaigns for two main demands: 1) *abolition of the emergency decrees*, and 2) *realization of the de Man* [12] *Plan.* The first issue is very important. The preceding government issued 150 reactionary emergency decrees, which are an extremely heavy burden on the working people. They were expected to be repealed at once. This was the demand of the Socialist Party. But have many of these emergency decrees been repealed by the new government? It has not repealed a single one. It has only mollified somewhat a few of the emergency decrees in order to make a sort of "token payment" in settlement of the generous promises of the Belgian Socialist leaders (like that "token dollar" which some European powers proffered the USA in payment of the millions due as war debts).

As regards the realization of the widely advertized de Man Plan, the matter has taken a turn quite unexpected by the

Social Democratic masses. The Socialist ministers announced that *the economic crisis must be overcome first* and only those provisions of the de Man Plan should be carried into effect which improve the position of the industrial capitalists and the banks; only afterwards would it be possible to adopt measures to improve the condition of the workers. But *how long* must the workers wait for their *share* in the "benefits" promised them in the de Man Plan? The Belgian bankers have already had their veritable *shower of gold.* The Belgian franc has been devalued 28 per cent; by this manipulation the bankers were able to pocket 4,500 million francs as their spoils at the expense of the wage earners and the savings of the small depositors. But how does this tally with the contents of the de Man Plan? Why, if we are to believe the letter of the plan, it promises to *"prosecute* monopolist abuses and speculative manipulations."

On the basis of the de Man Plan, the government has appointed a commission to supervise the banks. But the commission *consists of bankers* who can now gaily and lightheartedly supervise themselves.

The de Man Plan also promises a number of other good things, such as a *shorter working day, standardization of wages, a minimum wage, organization of an all-embracing system* of *social insurance*, "greater convenience in living conditions through new *housing construction,"* and so forth. These are all demands which we Communists can support. We should go to the labor organizations of Belgium and say to them: The capitalists have already received enough and even too much. Let us demand that the Social-Democratic ministers now carry out the promises they made to the workers. Let us get together in a *united front for the successful defense* of our interests. Minister Vandervelde, we support the demands on behalf of the workers contained in *your* platform; but we tell you frankly that we take these demands *seriously*, that we want action and not empty words, and therefore are rallying hundreds of thousands of workers to *struggle* for these demands.

Thus, in countries having Social-Democratic governments, the Communists, by utilizing appropriate individual demands taken from the platforms of the Social-Democratic ministers as a starting point for achieving joint action with the Social-Democratic Parties and organizations, can afterwards more easily develop a campaign for the establishment of a united front on the basis of other mass demands in the struggle against the capitalist offensive, against fascism and the threat of war.

It must further be borne in mind that, in general, joint action with the Social-Democratic Parties and organizations requires from Communists serious and substantiated criticism of Social Democracy as the ideology and practice of class collaboration with the bourgeoisie, and untiring, comradely explanation to the Social-Democratic workers of the program and slogans of Communism. In countries having Social-Democratic governments this task is of particular importance in the struggle for a united front.

The struggle for trade union unity

Comrades, a most important stage in the consolidation of the united front must be the establishment of national and international trade union unity.

As you know, the splitting tactics of the reformist leaders were applied most virulently in the trade unions. The reason for this is clear. Here their policy of class collaboration with the bourgeoisie found its practical culmination directly in the factories, to the detriment of the vital interests of the working class. This, of course, gave rise to sharp criticism and resistance on the part of the revolutionary workers under the leadership of the Communists. That is why the struggle between communism and reformism raged most fiercely in the trade unions.

The more difficult and complicated the situation became for capitalism, the more reactionary was the policy of the leaders of the Amsterdam trade unions, *[The International Federation of Trade Unions (IFTU), based in Amsterdam]* and the more aggressive their measures against all opposition elements within the trade unions. Even the establishment of the fascist dictatorship in Germany and the intensified capitalist offensive in all capitalist countries failed to diminish this aggressiveness. Is it not a characteristic fact that in 1933 alone, most disgraceful circulars were issued for the expulsion of Communists and revolutionary workers from the trade unions in Great Britain, Holland, Belgium and Sweden?

In Great Britain a circular was issued in 1933 prohibiting the local branches of the trade unions from joining anti-war or other revolutionary organizations. That was a prelude to the notorious "Black Circular" of the Trade Union Congress General Council, which outlawed any trade councils admitting delegates "directly or indirectly associated with Communist organizations." What is there left to be said of the leadership of the German trade unions, which applied unprecedented repressive measures against the revolutionary elements in the trade unions?

Yet we must base our tactics, not on the behavior of individual leaders of the Amsterdam unions, no matter what difficulties their behavior may cause the class struggle, but primarily on the question of *where the masses of workers are to be found.* And here we must openly declare that work in the trade unions is the most vital question in the work of all the Communist Parties. We must bring about a real change for the better in trade union work and make the question of struggle for trade union unity the central issue.

Ignoring the urge of the workers to join the trade unions, and faced with the difficulties of working within the Amsterdam unions, many of our comrades decided to pass by this complicated task. They invariably spoke of an organizational crisis in the Amsterdam unions, of the workers deserting the unions, but failed to notice that after some decline at the beginning of the world economic crisis, these unions later began to grow again. A peculiarity of the trade union movement has been precisely the fact that the attacks of the bourgeoisie on trade union rights, the attempts in a number of countries to "coordinate" the trade unions (Poland, Hungary, etc.), the curtailment of social insurance, and the cutting of wages forced the workers, notwithstanding the lack of resistance on the part of the reformist trade union leaders, to rally still more closely around these unions, because the workers wanted and still want to see in the trade unions the militant champions of their vital class interests. This explains the fact that most of the Amsterdam unions -- in France, Czechoslovakia, Belgium,

Holland, Switzerland, Sweden, etc. -- have grown in membership during the last few years. The American Federation of Labor has also considerably increased its membership in the past two years.

Had the German comrades better understood the problem of trade union work of which Comrade Thaelmann spoke on many occasions, there would undoubtedly have been a better situation in the trade unions than was the case at the time the fascist dictatorship was established. At the end of 1932 only about ten percent of the Party members belonged to the free trade unions. This in spite of the fact that after the Sixth Congress of the Comintern the Communists took the lead in quite a number of strikes. Our comrades used to write in the press of the need to assign 90 per cent of our forces to work in the trade unions, but in reality activity was concentrated exclusively around the revolutionary trade union opposition, which actually sought to replace the trade unions. And how about the period after Hitler's seizure of power? For two years many of our comrades stubbornly and systematically opposed the correct slogan of fighting for the re-establishment of the free unions.

I could cite similar examples about almost every other capitalist country.

But we already have the first serious achievements to our credit in the struggle for trade union unity in European countries. I have in mind little Austria, where on the initiative of the Communist Party a basis has been created for an illegal trade union movement. After the February battles the Social-Democrats, with Otto Bauer at their head, issued the watchword: "The free unions can be re-established only after the downfall of fascism." The Communists applied themselves to the *task of reestablishing the trade unions.* Every phase of that work was a bit of the living united front of the Austrian proletariat. The successful re-establishment of the free trade unions in underground conditions was a serious blow to fascism. The Social-Democrats were at the parting of the ways. Some of them tried to negotiate with the government. Others, seeing our successes, created their own parallel illegal trade unions. But there could be only one road: *either capitulation to fascism, or towards trade union unity through joint struggle against fascism.* Under mass pressure, the wavering leadership of the parallel unions created by the former trade union leaders decided to agree to amalgamation. The basis of this amalgamation is irreconcilable struggle against the offensive of capitalism and fascism and the guarantee of trade union democracy. We welcome this fact of the amalgamation of the trade unions, which is the first of its kind since the formal split of the trade unions after the war and which is therefore of *international importance.*

In *France* the united front has unquestionably served as a mighty impetus for achieving trade union unity. The leaders of the General Confederation of Labor have hampered and still hamper in every way the realization of unity, countering the main issue of the class policy of the trade unions by raising issues of a subordinate and secondary or formal character. An unquestionable success in the struggle for trade union unity has been the establishment of *single unions* on a local scale embracing, in the case of the railroad workers, for instance, approximately three-quarters of the membership of both trade unions.

We are definitely for the re-establishment of *trade union unity in every country and on an international scale.*

We are for one union in every industry. We are for one federation of trade unions in every country

We are for single international federations of trade unions organized by industries.

We stand for one international of trade unions based on

80

the class struggle.

We are for united class trade unions as one of the major bulwarks of the working class against the offensive of capital and fascism. Our only condition for uniting the trade unions is: *Struggle against capital, against fascism and for internal trade union democracy.*

Time does not wait. To us the question of trade union unity on a national as well as international scale is a question of the great task of uniting our class in mighty single trade union organizations against the class enemy. We welcome the fact that on the eve of May Day of this year the Red International of Labor Unions approached the Amsterdam International with the proposal to consider jointly the question of the terms, methods and forms of uniting the world trade union movement. The leaders of the Amsterdam International rejected that proposal, using the outworn pretext that unity in the trade union movement is possible only within the Amsterdam International, which, by the way, includes trade unions in only a part of the European countries.

But the communists working in the trade unions must continue to struggle tirelessly for the unity of the trade union movement. The task of the Red Trade Unions and the R.I.L.U. is to do all in their power to hasten the achievement of a joint struggle of all trade unions against the offensive of capital and fascism, and to bring about unity in the trade union movement, despite the stubborn resistance of the reactionary leaders of the Amsterdam International. The Red Trade Unions and the R.I.L.U must receive our unstinted support along this line.

In countries where small Red trade unions exist, we recommend working for their inclusion in the big reformist unions, but demanding the right to defend their views and the reinstatement of expelled members. But in countries where big Red trade unions exist parallel with big reformist trade unions, we must work for the convening of *unity congresses* on the basis of a platform of struggle against the capitalist offensive and the guarantee of *trade union democracy.*

It should be stated categorically that any Communist worker, any revolutionary worker who does not belong to the mass trade union of his industry, who does not fight to transform the reformist trade union into a real class trade union organization, who does not fight for trade union unity on the basis of the class struggle, such a Communist worker, such a revolutionary worker, does not discharge his elementary proletarian duty.

The United Front and the youth

Comrades, I have already pointed out the role played in the victory of fascism by the enlistment of the youth in the fascist organizations. In speaking of the youth, we must state frankly that we have neglected our task of drawing the masses of the working youth into the struggle against the offensive of capital, against fascism and the danger of war; we have neglected this task in a number of countries. We have underestimated the enormous importance of the youth in the fight against fascism. We have not always taken into account the special economic, political and cultural interests of the youth. We have likewise not paid proper attention to the revolutionary education of the youth.

All this has been utilized very cleverly by fascism, which in some countries, particularly in Germany, has inveigled large sections of the youth onto the anti-proletarian road. It should be borne in mind that it is not only by the glamor of militarism that fascism entices the youth. It feeds and clothes some of them in its detachments, gives work to others, and even sets up so-called cultural institutions for the youth, trying in this way to imbue them with the idea that it really can and wants to feed, clothe, teach and provide work for the mass of the working youth.

In a number of capitalist countries our Young Communist Leagues are still mainly sectarian organizations divorced from the masses. Their fundamental weakness is that they still try to copy the Communist Parties, to copy their forms and methods of work, forgetting that the YCL is *not a Communist party of the youth*. They do not take sufficient account of the fact that it is an organization with its own special tasks. Its methods and forms of work, education and struggle must be adapted to the actual level and needs of the youth.

Our Young Communists have shown memorable examples of heroism in the fight against fascist violence and bourgeois reaction. But they still lack the ability to win the masses of the youth away from hostile influences by dint of stubborn concrete work, as is evident from the fact that they have not yet overcome their opposition to work in the fascist mass organizations, and that their approach to the Socialist youth and other non-Communist youth is not always correct.

A great part of the responsibility for all this must be borne, of course, by the Communist parties as well, for they ought to lead and support the YCL in its work. For the problem of the youth is not only a YCL problem. *It is a problem for the whole Communist movement.* In the struggle for the youth, the Communist Parties and the YCL organizations must effect a genuine decisive change. The main task of the Communist youth movement in capitalist countries is to advance boldly in the direction of bringing about a *united* front along the path of organizing and rallying the young generation of working people. The tremendous influence that even the first steps taken in this direction exert on the revolutionary movement of the youth is shown by the examples of *France* and the *United States* during the recent past. It was sufficient in these countries to proceed to apply the united front for considerable successes to be immediately achieved. In the sphere of the international united front, the successful initiative of the committee against war and fascism in Paris in bringing about the international cooperation of all *non-fascist* youth organizations is also worthy of note in this connection.

These recent successful steps in the united front movement of the youth also show that the forms which the united front of the youth should assume must not be stereotyped, nor necessarily be the same as those met with in the practice of the Communist parties. The Young Communist Leagues must strive in every way to unite the forces of all non-fascist mass organizations of the youth, including the formation of various kinds of common organizations for the struggle against fascism, against the unprecedented manner in which the youth is being stripped of every right, against the militarization of the youth and for the economic and cultural rights of the young generation, in order to draw these young workers over to the side of the anti-fascist front, no matter where they may be -- in the factories, the forced labor camps, the labor exchanges, the army barracks and the fleet, the schools, or in the various sports, cultural or other organizations.

In developing and strengthening the YCL, our YCL members must work for the formation of anti-fascist associations of the Communist and Socialist Youth Leagues on a platform of class struggle.

The United Front and women

Comrades, work among working women - among women workers, unemployed women, peasant women and housewives -- has been underestimated no less than work among the youth. While fascism exacts most of all from youth, it enslaves women with particular ruthlessness and cynicism, playing on the innermost feelings of the mother, housewife, the single working woman, uncertain of the morrow. Fascism, posing as a benefactor, throws the starving family a few beggarly scarps, trying in this way to stifle the bitterness aroused, particularly among the working women by the unprecedented slavery which fascism brings them. It drives working women out of industry, forcibly sends needy girls into the country, dooming them to the position of unpaid servants of rich farmers and landlords. While promising women a happy home and family life, it drives women to prostitution more than any other capitalist regime.

Communists, above all our women Communists, must remember that there cannot be a successful fight against fascism and war unless the wide masses of women are drawn into the struggle. Agitation alone will not accomplish this. Taking into account the concrete situation in each instance, we must find a way of mobilizing the mass of women by work around their vital interests and demands-in a fight for their demands against high prices, for higher wages on the basis of the principle of equal pay for equal work, against mass dismissals, against every manifestation of inequality in the status of women and against fascist enslavement.

In endeavoring to draw women who work into the revolutionary movement, we must not be afraid of forming separate women's organizations for this purpose, wherever necessary. The preconceived notion that the women's organizations under Communist party leadership in the capitalist countries should be abolished as part of the struggle against 'women's separatism' in the labor movement, has often done great harm.

The simplest and most flexible forms should be sought to establish contact and a joint struggle between the revolutionary, Social-Democratic and progressive antiwar and anti-fascist women's organizations. We must spare no pains to see that the women workers and working women in general fight shoulder to shoulder with their class brothers in the ranks of the united working-class front and the anti-fascist People's Front.

The anti-imperialist United Front

The changed international and internal situation lends exceptional importance to the question of *the anti-imperialist united front* in all colonial and semi-colonial countries.

In forming a broad anti-imperialist united front of struggle in the colonies and semi-colonies it is necessary above all to recognize the variety of conditions in which the anti-imperialist struggle of the masses is proceeding, the varying degree of maturity of the national liberation movement, the role of the proletariat within it and the influence of the Communist party over the masses.

In Brazil the problem differs from that in India, China and other countries.

In *Brazil* the Communist Party, having laid a correct foundation for the development of the united anti-imperialist front by the establishment of the National Liberation Alliance, [13] must make every effort to extend this front by drawing into it first and foremost the many millions of the peasantry, leading up to the formation of units of a people's revolutionary army, completely devoted to the revolution and to the establishment of a government of the National Liberation Alliance.

In *India* the Communists must support, extend and participate in all anti-imperialist mass activities, not excluding those which are under national reformist leadership. While maintaining their political organizational independence, they must carry on active work inside the organizations which take part in the Indian National Congress, facilitating the process of crystallization of a national revolutionary wing among them, for the purpose of further developing the national liberation movement of the Indian peoples against British imperialism.

In *China*, where the people's movement has already led to the formation of soviet districts over a considerable territory of the country and to the organization of a powerful Red Army, the predatory offensive of Japanese imperialism and the treason of the Nanking government have brought into jeopardy the national existence of the great Chinese people. The Chinese soviets act as a unifying center in the struggle against the enslavement and partition of China by the imperialists, as a unifying center which will rally all anti-imperialist forces for the national defense of the Chinese people.

We therefore approve the initiative taken by our courageous brother Party of China in the creation of a most extensive anti-imperialist united front against Japanese imperialism and its Chinese agents, jointly with all those organized forces existing on the territory of China which are ready to wage a real struggle for the salvation of their country and their people. I am sure that I express the sentiments and thoughts of our entire Congress in saying that we send our warmest fraternal greetings, in the name of the revolutionary proletariat of the whole world, to all the soviets in China, to the Chinese revolutionary people. We send our ardent fraternal greetings to the heroic Red Army of China, tried in a thousand battles. And we assure the Chinese people of our firm resolve to support its struggle for its complete liberation from all imperialist robbers and their Chinese henchmen.

A United Front government

Comrades, we have taken a bold, resolute course towards the united front of the working class, and are ready to carry it out with full consistency.

If we Communists are asked whether we advocate the united front *only* in the fight for partial demands, or whether we are prepared to share the responsibility even when it will be a question of forming a government on the basis of the united front, then we say with a full sense of our responsibility: Yes, we recognize that a situation may arise in which the formation of a *government of the proletarian united front*, or of an *anti-fascist People's Front*, will become not only possible but necessary. And in that case we shall advocate for the formation of such a government without the slightest hesitation.

I am not speaking here of a government which may be formed *after* the victory of the proletarian revolution. It is not impossible, of course, that in some country, immediately after the revolutionary overthrow of the bourgeoisie, there may be formed a government on the basis of a government bloc of the Communist party with a certain party (or its Left wing) participating in the revolution. After the October Revolution the victorious party of the Russian Bolsheviks, as we know, included representatives of the Left Socialist-Revolutionaries in the Soviet Government. This was a specific feature of the first Soviet government after the victory of the October Revolution.

I am not speaking of such a case, but of the possible formation of a united front government on the eve of and before the victory of the revolution.

What kind of government is this? And in what situation

could there be any question of such a government?

It is primarily a *government of struggle against fascism and reaction.* It must be a government arising as the result of the united front movement and in no way restricting the activity of the Communist party and the mass organizations of the working class, but on the contrary, taking resolute measures against the counterrevolutionary financial magnates and their fascist agents.

At a suitable moment, relying on the growing united front movement, the Communist Party of a given country will advocate the formation of such a government on the basis of a definite anti-fascist platform.

Under what objective conditions will it be possible to form such a government? In the most general terms, one can reply to this question as follows: under conditions of a *political crisis*, when the ruling classes are no longer able to cope with the powerful rise of the mass anti-fascist movement. But this is only a general perspective, without which it will scarcely be possible in practice to form a united front government. Only the existence of certain *special prerequisites* can put on the agenda the question of forming such government as a politically essential task. It seems to me that the following prerequisites deserve the greatest attention in this connection:

First, the state apparatus of the bourgeoisie must already be sufficiently *disorganized and paralyzed*, so that the bourgeoisie cannot prevent the formation of a government of struggle against reaction and fascism.

Second, the widest masses of working people, particularly the mass trade unions, must be in a state of vehement revolt *against fascism and reaction*, though *not ready* to rise in insurrection so as to *fight under Communist Party leadership for the establishment of a fully socialist government.*

Third, the differentiation and radicalization in the ranks

of Social-Democracy and other parties participating in the united front must already have reached the point where a considerable proportion of them demand *ruthless measures against the fascists and other reactionaries*, fight together with the Communists against fascism and openly oppose the reactionary section of their own party which is hostile to Communism.

When and in what countries a situation will actually arise in which these prerequisites will be present in a sufficient degree, it is impossible to state in advance. But as such a possibility *is not to be ruled out in any of the capitalist countries*, we must reckon with it, and not only so orient and prepare ourselves, but also orient the working class accordingly.

The fact that we are bringing up this question for discussion at all today is, of course, connected with our estimate of the situation and immediate prospects, as well as with the actual growth of the united front movement in a number of countries during the recent past. For more than ten years the situation in the capitalist countries was such that it was not necessary for the Communist International to discuss a question of this kind.

You remember, Comrades, that at our Fourth Congress in 1922, and again at the Fifth Congress in 1924, the question of the slogan of a *workers', or a workers' and peasants' government* was under discussion. Originally the issue turned essentially upon a question was almost comparable to the one we are discussing today. The debates that took place at that time in the Communist International around this question, and in particular the political *errors* which were committed in connection with it, have to this day retained their importance for *sharpening our vigilance against the danger of deviations to the "Right" or "Left"* from *the Bolshevik line* on this question. Therefore I shall briefly point out a few of these errors, in order to draw from them the lessons necessary for the present policy of our Parties.

The first series of mistakes arose from the fact that the question of a workers' government was not clearly and firmly bound up with the existence of a political crisis. Owing to this, the Right opportunists were able to interpret matters as though we should strive for the formation of a workers' government, supported by the Communist party, in any, so to speak, "normal" situation. The ultra-Lefts, on the other hand, recognized only a workers' government formed by an armed insurrection after the overthrow of the bourgeoisie. Both views were wrong. In order, therefore, to avoid a repetition of such mistakes, we now *lay great stress on the exact consideration* of the specific, concrete circumstances of the political crisis and the upsurge of the mass movement, in which the formation of a united front government may prove possible and politically necessary.

The second series of errors arose from the fact that the question of a workers' government was not bound up with the development of a militant mass *united front movement of the proletariat.* Thus the Right opportunists were able to distort the question, reducing it to the unprincipled tactics of forming blocs with Social-Democratic Parties on the basis of purely parliamentary combinations.

The ultra-Lefts, on the contrary, shrieked: "No coalitions with counter-revolutionary Social-Democrats!" -- considering all Social-Democrats as essentially counterrevolutionary.

Both were wrong, and we now emphasize, on the one hand, that we are not in the least anxious for a workers government" that would be nothing more nor less than an enlarged Social-Democratic government. We even prefer not to use the term "workers' government," and *speak of a united front government,* which in political character is something absolutely different, *different in principle,* from all the Social-Democratic governments which usually call themselves "workers' (or labor) government." While the Social-Democratic government is an instrument of class collaboration with the bourgeoisie in the interests of the preservation of the capitalist order, a united front government is an instrument of the collaboration of the revolutionary vanguard of the proletariat with other anti-fascist parties, in the interests of the entire working population, a government of struggle against fascism and reaction. Obviously there is a *radical difference* between these two things.

On the other hand, we stress the need to see *the difference between the two different camps of Social-Democracy.* As I have already pointed out, there is a reactionary camp of Social-Democracy, but alongside with it there exists and is growing the camp of the Left Social-Democrats (without quotation marks), of workers who are becoming revolutionary. In practice the decisive difference between them consists in their attitude towards the united front of the working class. The reactionary Social-Democrats are *against* the united front; they slander the united front movement, they sabotage and disintegrate it, as it undermines their policy of compromise with the bourgeoisie. The Left Social-Democrats are *for the united front;* they defend, develop and strengthen the united front movement. Inasmuch as this united front movement is a militant movement against fascism and reaction, it will be a constant driving force, impelling the united front government to struggle against the reactionary bourgeoisie. The more powerful this mass movement, the greater the force with which it can back the government in combating the reactionaries. And the better this mass movement will be organized *from below*, the wider the network of *non-party class organs of the united front in the factories*, among *the unemployed*, in *the workers' districts*, among *the people of town and country*, the greater will be the guarantee against a possible degeneration of the policy of the united front government.

The third series of mistaken views which came to light during our former debates touched precisely on the practical policy of the "workers' government." The right opportunists considered that a "workers' government" ought to keep "within the framework of bourgeois democracy," and consequently ought not to take any steps going beyond this framework. The ultra-Lefts, on the other hand, in practice refused to make any attempt to form a united front government.

In 1923 Saxony and Thuringia presented a clear picture of a Right opportunist "workers' government" in action. The entry of the Communists into the Workers' Government of Saxony jointly with the Left Social-Democrats (Ziegner group) was no mistake in itself; on the contrary, the revolutionary situation in Germany fully justified this step. But in taking part in the government, the Communists should have used their positions primarily *for the purpose of arming the proletariat.* This they did not do. They did not even requisition a single apartment of the rich, although the housing shortage among the workers was so great that many of them with their wives and children were still without a roof over their heads. They also did *nothing* to organize the revolutionary mass movement of the workers. They behaved in general like *ordinary* parliamentary ministers "within the framework of bourgeois democracy." As you know, this was the result of the opportunist policy of Brandler and his adherents. The result was such bankruptcy that to this day we have to refer to the government of Saxony as the classical example of how revolutionaries *should not behave* when in office.

Comrades, we demand an entirely different policy from a united front government. We demand that it should carry out *definite and fundamental revolutionary demands* required by the situation. For instance, control of production, control of the banks, disbanding of the police and its replacement by an armed workers' militia, etc.

Fifteen years ago Lenin called upon us to focus all our attention on "searching out forms of *transition* or *approach* to the proletariat revolution." It may be that in a number of countries *the united front government* will prove to be *one* of the most important transitional forms.

"Left" doctrinaires have always avoided this precept of Lenin's. Like the narrow-minded propagandists that they were, they spoke only of aims, without ever worrying about "forms of transition." The Right Opportunists, on the other hand, have tried to establish a *special democratic intermediate stage* lying between the dictatorship of the bourgeoisie and the dictatorship of the proletariat, for the purpose of instilling into the workers the illusion of a peaceful parliamentary passage from the one dictatorship to the other. This fictitious "intermediate stage" they have also called "transitional form," and even quoted Lenin's words. But this piece of swindling was not difficult to expose: for Lenin spoke of the form of transition and approach to *the proletarian revolution*, that is, to the overthrow of the bourgeois dictatorship, and not of some transitional form *between* the bourgeois and the proletarian dictatorship.

Why did Lenin attach such exceptionally great importance to the form of transition to the proletarian revolution? Because he had in mind *the fundamental law of all great revolutions*, the law that for the masses propaganda and agitation alone cannot take the place of *their own political experience*, when it is a question of attracting really broad masses of the working people to the side of the revolutionary vanguard, without which a victorious struggle for power is impossible. It is a common mistake of a Leftist character to imagine that as soon as a political (or revolutionary) crisis arises, it is enough for the Communist leaders to put forth the slogan of revolutionary insurrection, and the broad masses will follow them. No, even in such a crisis the masses are by no means always ready to do so. We saw this in the case of Spain.

97

To help *the millions* to master as rapidly as possible, through their own experience, what they have to do, where to find a radical solution, and what Party is worthy of their confidence -- these among others are the purposes for which both transitional slogans and special "forms of *transition or approach* to the proletarian revolution" are necessary. Otherwise the great mass of the people, who are under the influence of petty bourgeois democratic illusions and traditions, may waver even when there is a revolutionary situation, may procrastinate and stray, without finding the road to revolution -- and then come under the ax of the fascist executioners.

That is why we indicate the possibility of forming an anti-fascist united front government in the conditions of a political crisis. In so far as such a government will really prosecute the struggle against the enemies of the people, and give a free hand to the working class and the Communist party, we Communists shall accord it our unstinted support, and as soldiers of the revolution shall take our place *in the first line of fire*. But we state frankly to the masses:

Final salvation this government cannot bring. It is not in a position to overthrow the class rule of the exploiters, and for this reason cannot finally remove the danger of fascist counter-revolution. Consequently *it is necessary to prepare for the socialist revolution.*

In estimating the present development of the world situation, we see that *a political crisis* is maturing in quite a number of countries. This makes a firm decision by our Congress on the question of a united front government a matter of great urgency and importance.

If our parties are able to utilize in a Bolshevik fashion the opportunity of forming a united front government and of waging the struggle for the formation and maintenance in power of such a government, *for the revolutionary training of the masses*, this will be *the best political justification* in our policy

98

in favor of the formation of united front governments.

The ideological struggle against fascism

One of the weakest aspects of the anti-fascist struggle of our Parties is that *they react inadequately and too slowly to the demagogy of fascism*, and to this day continue to neglect the problems of the struggle against fascist ideology. Many comrades did not believe that so reactionary a brand of bourgeois ideology as the ideology of fascism, which in its stupidity frequently reaches the point of lunacy, would be able to gain any mass influence. This was a serious mistake. The putrefaction of capitalism penetrates to the innermost core of its ideology and culture, while the desperate situation of wide masses of the people renders certain sections of them susceptible to infection from the ideological refuse of this putrefaction.

Under no circumstances must we underrate fascism's power of ideological infection. On the contrary, we for our part must develop an extensive ideological struggle based on clear, popular arguments and a correct, well thought out approach to the peculiarities of the national psychology of the masses of the people.

The fascists are rummaging through the entire *history* of every nation so as to be able to pose as the heirs and continuators of all that was exalted and heroic in its past, while all that was degrading or offensive to the national sentiments of the people they make use of as weapons against the enemies of fascism. Hundreds of books are being published in Germany with only one aim -- to falsify the history of the German people and give it a fascist complexion. The new-baked National Socialist historians try to depict the history of Germany as if for the past two thousand years, by virtue of some historical law, a certain line of development had run through it like a red thread, leading to the appearance on the historical scene of a national 'savior', a 'Messiah' of the German people, a certain 'Corporal' of Austrian extraction. In these books the greatest figures of the German people of the past are represented as having been fascists, while the great peasant movements are set down as the direct precursors of the fascist movement.

Mussolini does his utmost to make capital for himself out of the heroic figure of Garibaldi. The French fascists bring to the fore as their heroine Joan of Arc. The American fascists appeal to the traditions of the American War of Independence, the traditions of Washington and Lincoln. The Bulgarian fascists make use of the national-liberation movement of the seventies and its heroes beloved by the people, Vassil Levsky, Stephan Karaj and others.

Communists who suppose that all this has nothing to do with the cause of the working class, who do nothing to enlighten the masses on the past of their people in a historically correct fashion, in a genuinely Marxist-Leninist spirit, who do nothing *to link up the present struggle with the people's revolutionary traditions and* past -- voluntarily hand over to the fascist falsifiers all that is valuable in the historical past of the nation, so that the fascists may fool the masses.

No, Comrades, *we are concerned with every important question, not only of the present and the future, but also of the past of our own peoples.* We Communists do not pursue a narrow policy based on the craft interests of the workers. We are not narrow-minded trade union functionaries, or leaders of medieval guilds of handicraftsmen and journeymen. We are the representatives of the class interests of the most important, the greatest class of modern society-the working class, to whose destiny it falls to free mankind from the sufferings of the capitalist system, the class which in one-sixth of the world has already cast off the yoke of capitalism and constitutes the ruling class. We defend the vital interests of all the exploited, toiling strata, that is, of the overwhelming majority in any capitalist country.

We Communists are the *irreconcilable opponents, in principle*, of bourgeois nationalism in all its forms. But *we are not supporters of national nihilism*, and should never act as such. The task of educating the workers and all working people in the spirit of proletarian internationalism is one of the fundamental tasks of every Communist Party. But anyone who thinks that this permits him, or even compels him, to sneer at all the national sentiments of the broad masses of working people is far from being a genuine Bolshevik, and has understood nothing of the teaching of Lenin on the national question.

Lenin, who always fought bourgeois nationalism resolutely and consistently, gave us an example of the correct approach to the problem of national sentiments in his article "On the National Pride of the Great Russians" written in 1914. He wrote:

Are we class-conscious Great-Russian proletarians impervious to the feeling of national pride? Certainly not. We love our language and our motherland; we, more than any other group, are working to raise its laboring masses (i.e., nine-tenths of its population) to the level of intelligent democrats and socialists. We, more than anybody are grieved to see and feel to what violence, oppression and mockery our beautiful motherland is being subjected by the tsarist hangmen, the nobles and the capitalists. We are proud of the fact that those acts of violence met with resistance in our midst, in the midst of the Great Russians; that this midst brought forth Radischev, the Decembrists, the intellectual revolutionaries of the seventies; that in 1905 the Great-Russian working class created a powerful revolutionary party of the masses. .

We are filled with national pride because of the knowledge that the Great-Russian nation, *too*, has created a revolutionary class, that it, too, has proved capable of giving humanity great examples of struggle for freedom and for socialism; that its contribution is not confined solely to great pogroms, numerous scaffolds, torture chambers, severe famines and abject servility before the priests, the tsars, the landowners and the capitalists.

We are filled with national pride, and therefore we *particularly* hate *our* slavish past... and our slavish present, in which the same landowners, aided by the capitalists, lead us into war to stifle Poland and the Ukraine, to throttle the democratic movement in Persia and in China, to strengthen the gang of Romanovs, Bobrinskis, Puriskeviches that cover with shame our Great-Russian national dignity. *[V. I. Lenin, Collected Works 21:103-4]*

This is what Lenin wrote on national pride.

I think, comrades, that when at the Reichstag Fire Trial the fascists tried to slander the Bulgarians as a barbarous people, I was not wrong in taking up the defense of the national honor of the working masses of the Bulgarian people, who are struggling heroically against the fascist usurpers, the real barbarians and savages, nor was I wrong in declaring that I had no cause to be ashamed of being a Bulgarian, but that, on the contrary, I was proud of being a son of the heroic Bulgarian working class.

Comrades, proletarian internationalism must, so to speak, "acclimatize itself" in each country in order to strike deep roots in its native land. *National forms* of the proletarian class struggle and of the labor movement in the individual countries are in no contradiction to proletarian internationalism; on the contrary, it is precisely in these forms that *the international interests of the proletariat* can be successfully defended.

It goes without saying that it is necessary *everywhere*

and on all occasions to expose before the masses and prove to them concretely that the fascist bourgeoisie, on the pretext of defending general national interests, is conducting its selfish policy of oppressing and exploiting its own people, as well as robbing and enslaving other nations. But *we must not confine ourselves to this.* We must at the same time prove by the very struggle of the working class and the actions of the Communist Parties that the proletariat, in rising against every manner of bondage and national oppression, is the *only* true fighter for national freedom and the independence of the people.

The interests of the class struggle of the proletariat against its native exploiters and oppressors are not in contradiction to the interests of a free and happy future of the nation. On the contrary, the socialist revolution will signify *the salvation of the nation* and will open up to it the road to loftier heights. By the *very fact* of building at the present time its class organizations and consolidating its positions, by the very fact of defending democratic rights and liberties against fascism, by the *very fact* of fighting for the overthrow of capitalism, the working class is fighting for the future of the nation.

The revolutionary proletariat is fighting to save the culture of the people, to liberate it from the shackles of decaying monopoly capitalism, from barbarous fascism, which is laying violent hands on it. *Only* the proletarian revolution can avert the destruction of culture and raise it to its highest flowering as a truly national culture -- *national in form and socialist in content* -- which is being realized in the Union of Soviet Socialist Republics before our very eyes.

Proletarian internationalism not only is not in contradiction to this struggle of the working people of the individual countries for national, social and cultural freedom, but, thanks to international proletarian solidarity and fighting unity, assures *the support* that is necessary for victory in this struggle. The working class in the capitalist countries can triumph *only in the closest alliance* with the victorious proletariat of the great Soviet Union. *Only* by struggling hand in hand with the proletariat of the imperialist countries can the colonial peoples and oppressed national minorities achieve their freedom. The *sole* road to victory for the proletarian revolution in the imperialist countries lies through the revolutionary alliance of the working class of the imperialist countries with the national-liberation movement in the colonies and dependent countries, because, as *Marx* taught us, "no nation can be free if it oppresses other nations."

Communists belonging to an oppressed, dependent nation cannot combat chauvinism successfully among the people of their own nation if they do not *at the same time show* in practice, in the mass movement, that they actually struggle for the liberation of their nation from the alien yoke. And again, on the other hand, the Communists of an oppressing nation cannot do what is necessary to educate the working masses of their nation in the spirit of internationalism *without waging* a resolute struggle against the oppressor policy of their "own" bourgeoisie, for the right of complete self-determination for the nations kept in bondage by it. If they do not do this, they likewise do not make it easier for the working people of the oppressed nation to overcome their nationalist prejudices.

If we act in this spirit, if in all our mass work we prove convincingly that we are free of both national nihilism and bourgeois nationalism, then and only then shall we be able to wage a really successful struggle against the jingo demagogy of the fascists.

That is the reason why a correct and practical application of the Leninist national policy is of such paramount importance. It is *unquestionably an essential* preliminary condition for a successful struggle against chauvinism -- this main instrument of ideological influence of the fascists upon the masses.

III. CONSOLIDATION OF THE COMMUNIST PARTIESAND THE STRUGGLE FOR POLITICAL UNITY OF THE PROLETARIAT

Comrades, in the struggle to establish a united front the importance of the leading role of the Communist Party increases extraordinarily. Only the Communist Party is at bottom the initiator, the organizer and the driving force of the united front of the working class.

The Communist Parties can ensure the mobilization of the broadest masses of working people for a united struggle against fascism and the offensive of capital *only if they strengthen their own ranks in every respect*, if they develop their initiative, pursue a Marxist-Leninist policy and apply correct, flexible tactics which take into account the actual situation and alignment of class forces.

Consolidation of the Communist parties

In the period between the Sixth and Seventh Congress, our Parties in the capitalist countries have undoubtedly *grown in stature and have been considerably steeled.* But it would be a most dangerous mistake to rest content with this achievement. The more the united front of the working class extends, the more will new, complex problems arise before us and the more will it be necessary for us to work on the political and organizational consolidation of our Parties. The united front of the proletariat brings to the fore an army of workers who will be able to carry out their mission if this army is headed by a leading force that will point out its aims and paths. This leading force can *only be a strong proletarian, revolutionary party.*

If we Communists exert every effort to establish a united front, we do this not for the narrow purpose of recruiting new members for the Communist Parties. But we must strengthen the Communist Parties in every way and increase their membership for the very reason that we seriously want to strengthen the united front. The strengthening of the Communist Parties is not a narrow Party concern but the concern of the entire working class.

The unity, revolutionary solidarity and fighting preparedness of the Communist Parties constitute a most valuable capital which belongs not only to us but to the whole working class. We have combined and shall continue to combine our readiness to march jointly with the Social-Democratic Parties and organizations to the struggle against fascism with an irreconcilable struggle against Social-Democracy as the ideology and practice of compromise with the bourgeoisie, and consequently also against any penetration of this ideology into our own ranks.

In boldly and resolutely carrying out the policy of the united front, we meet in our own ranks with obstacles which we must remove at all costs in the shortest possible time.

After the Sixth Congress of the Communist International, a successful struggle was waged in all Communist Parties of the capitalist countries against any tendency towards an opportunist adaptation to the conditions of capitalist stabilization and against any infection with reformist and legalist illusions. Our Parties purged their ranks of various kinds of Right opportunists, thus strengthening their Bolshevik unity and fighting capacity. Less successful, and frequently entirely lacking, was the fight against sectarianism. Sectarianism no longer manifested itself in primitive, open forms, as in the first years of the existence of the Communist International, but, under cover of a formal recognition of the Bolshevik theses, hindered the development of a Bolshevik mass policy. In our day this is often no longer an "infantile disorder," as Lenin wrote, but a *deeply rooted vice*, which must be shaken off or it will be impossible to solve the problem of establishing the united front of the proletariat and of leading the masses from the positions of reformism to the side of revolution.

In the present situation sectarianism, *self-satisfied* sectarianism, as we designate it in the draft resolution, more than anything else impedes our struggle for the realization of the united front: sectarianism, satisfied with its *doctrinaire narrowness*, its divorce from the real life of the masses, satisfied with its *simplified methods* of solving the most complex problems of the working class movement on the basis of stereotyped schemes; sectarianism which professes to know all and considers it superfluous to learn from the masses, from the lessons of the labor movement; in short, sectarianism, to which as they say, mountains are mere stepping-stones.

Self-satisfied sectarianism *will not and cannot*

110

understand that the leadership of the working class by the Communist Party does not come of itself. The leading role of the Communist Party in the struggles of the working class must be won. For this purpose it is necessary, not to rant about the leading role of the Communists, but *to earn and win the confidence of the working masses* by everyday mass work and a correct policy. This will be possible only if in our political work we Communists seriously take into account the actual level of the class consciousness of the masses, the degree to which they have become revolutionized, if we soberly appraise the actual situation, not on the basis of our wishes but on the basis of the actual state of affairs. Patiently, step by step, we must make it easier for the broad masses to come over to the Communist position. We ought never to forget the words of Lenin, who warns us as strongly as possible:

... This is the whole point -- we must not regard that which is obsolete for us, as obsolete for the class, as obsolete for   the   masses.
[V. I. Lenin, "Left-Wing" Communism, an Infantile Disorder, New York (1940), pp. 42; Collected Works 31:58]

Is it not a fact, comrades, that in our ranks there are still quite a few such doctrinaire elements, who at all times and places sense nothing but danger in the policy of the united front? For such comrades the whole united front is one unrelieved peril. But this sectarian "sticking to principle" is nothing but political helplessness in face of the difficulties of directly leading the struggle of the masses.

Sectarianism finds expression *particularly* in overestimating the revolutionization of the masses, in overestimating the speed at which they are abandoning the positions of reformism, and in attempting to leap over difficult stages and the complicated tasks of the movement. In practice, methods of leading the masses have frequently been replaced by the methods of leading a narrow party group. The strength of the traditional tie-up between the masses and their organizations and leaders was underestimated, and when the masses did not break off these connections, immediately the attitude taken toward them was just as harsh as that adopted toward their reactionary leaders. Tactics and slogans have tended to become stereotyped for all countries, the special features of the actual situation in each individual country being left out of account. The necessity of stubborn struggle in the very midst of the masses themselves to win their confidence has been ignored, the struggle for the partial demands of the workers and work in the reformist trade unions and fascist mass organizations have been neglected. The policy of the united front has frequently been replaced by bare appeals and abstract propaganda.

In no less a degree have sectarian views hindered the correct selection of people, the training and developing of *cadres connected* with the masses, *enjoying* the confidence of the masses, cadres *whose revolutionary mettle has been tried and tested* in class battles, cadres capable of combining *the practical experience of mass* work with a *Bolshevik staunchness of principle.*

Thus sectarianism has to a considerable extent retarded the growth of the Communist Parties, made it difficult to carry out a real mass policy, prevented our taking advantage of the difficulties of the class enemy to strengthen the positions of the revolutionary movement, and hindered the winning over of the broad masses of the proletariat to the side of the Communist Parties.

While fighting most resolutely to overcome and exterminate the last remnants of self-satisfied sectarianism, we must increase in every way our vigilance toward Right opportunism and the struggle against it and against every one of its concrete manifestations, bearing in mind that the danger of Right opportunism will increase in proportion as the broad united front develops. Already there are tendencies to reduce the role of the Communist Party in the ranks of the united front and to effect a reconciliation with Social-Democratic ideology. Nor must we lose sight of the fact that the tactics of the united front are a method of clearly convincing the Social-Democratic workers of the correctness of the Communist policy and the incorrectness of the reformist policy, and that they are *not a reconciliation with Social-Democratic ideology and practice.* A successful struggle to establish the united front imperatively demands constant struggle in our ranks against tendencies to *depreciate the role of the Party,* against *legalist illusions,* against reliance on spontaneity and *automatism,* both in liquidating fascism and in implementing the united front against *the slightest vacillation at the moment of decisive action.*

Political unity of the working class

Comrades, the development of the united front of joint struggle of the Communist and Social-Democratic workers against fascism and the offensive of capital also brings to the fore the question of *political unity*, of a *single political mass party of the working class*. The Social Democratic workers are becoming more and more convinced by experience that the struggle against the class enemy demands unity of political leadership, inasmuch as *duality in leadership* impedes the further development and reinforcement of the joint struggle of the working class.

The interests of the class struggle of the proletariat and the success of the proletarian revolution make it imperative that there be *a single party of the proletariat* in each country. Of course, it is not so easy or simple to achieve this. It requires stubborn work and struggle and is bound to be a more or less lengthy process. The Communist Parties, basing themselves on the growing urge of the workers for a unification of the Social-Democratic Parties or of individual organizations with the Communist Parties, must firmly and confidently take the initiative in this unification. The cause of amalgamating the forces of the working class in a single revolutionary proletarian party at the time when the international labor movement is entering the period of closing the split in its ranks, *is our cause.*

But while it is sufficient for the establishment of the united front of the Communist and Social-Democratic Parties to have an agreement to fight against fascism, the offensive of capital and war, the achievement of political unity is possible only on the basis of a number of certain conditions involving principles.

This unification is possible only on the following conditions:

- *First, complete independence from the bourgeoisie and dissolution of the bloc of Social-Democracy with the bourgeoisie;*
- *Second*, preliminary unity of action;
- *Third*, recognition of *the revolutionary overthrow of the rule of the bourgeoisie* and the establishment of the dictatorship *of the proletariat in the form of soviets* a sine qua non;
- *Fourth*, refusal to support one's own bourgeoisie in an *imperialist war;*
- *Fifth*, building up the Party on the basis of *democratic centralism*, which ensures unity of purpose and action, and which has been tested by the *experience of the Russian Bolsheviks.*

We must explain to the Social-Democratic workers, patiently and in comradely fashion, why political unity of the working class is impossible without these conditions. We must discuss together with them the sense and significance of these conditions.

Why is it necessary for the realization of the political unity of the proletariat that there be complete independence from the bourgeoisie and a rupture of the bloc of Social-Democrats with the bourgeoisie?

Because the whole experience of the labor movement, particularly the experience of the fifteen years of coalition policy in Germany, has shown that the policy of class collaboration, the policy of dependence on the bourgeoisie, leads to the defeat of the working class and to the victory of fascism. And the only true road to victory is the road of irreconcilable class struggle against the bourgeoisie, the road of the Bolsheviks.

Why must unity of action be first established as a preliminary condition of political unity?

Because unity of action to repel the offensive of capital and of fascism is possible and necessary even before the majority of the workers are united on a common political platform for the overthrow of capitalism, while the working out of unity of views on the main lines and aims of the struggle of the proletariat, without which a unification of the parties is impossible, requires a more or less extended period of time. And unity of views is worked out best of all in joint struggle against the class enemy already today. To propose to unite at once instead of forming a united front means to place the cart before the horse and to imagine that the cart will then move ahead. Precisely for the reason that for us the question of political unity is not a maneuver, as it is for many Social-Democratic leaders, we insist on the realization of unity of action as one of the most important stages in the struggle for political unity.

Why is it necessary to recognize the necessity of the revolutionary overthrow of the bourgeoisie and the setting up of the dictatorship of the proletariat in the form of soviet power?

Because the experience of the victory of the great October Revolution, on the one hand and, on the other, the bitter lessons learned in Germany, Austria and Spain during the entire postwar period have confirmed once more that the victory of the proletariat is possible only by means of the revolutionary overthrow of the bourgeoisie, and that the bourgeoisie would rather drown the labor movement in a sea of blood than allow the proletariat to establish socialism by peaceful means. The experience of the October Revolution has demonstrated patently that the basic content of the proletarian revolution is the question of the proletarian dictatorship, which is called upon to crush the resistance of the overthrown exploiters, to arm the revolution for the struggle against imperialism and to lead the revolution to the complete victory of socialism. To achieve the dictatorship of the proletariat as the dictatorship of the vast majority over an insignificant minority, over the exploiters -- and only as such can it be brought about -- for this soviets are needed embracing all sections of the working class, the basic masses of the peasantry and the rest of the working people, without whose awakening, without whose inclusion in the front of the revolutionary struggle, the victory of the proletariat cannot be consolidated.

Why is the refusal of support to the bourgeoisie in an imperialist war a condition of political unity?

Because the bourgeoisie wages imperialist wars for its predatory purposes, against the interests of the vast majority of the peoples, under whatever guise this war may be waged. Because all imperialists combine their feverish preparations for war with extremely intensified exploitation and oppression of the working people in their own country. Support of the bourgeoisie in such a war means treason to the country and the international working class.

Why, finally, is the building of the Party on the basis of democratic centralism a condition of unity?

Because only a party built on the basis of democratic centralism can ensure unity of purpose and action, can lead the proletariat to victory over the bourgeoisie, which has at its disposal so powerful a weapon as the centralized state apparatus. The application of the principle of democratic centralism has stood the splendid historical test of the experience of the Russian Bolshevik Party, the Party of Lenin.

This explains why it is necessary to strive for political unity on the basis of the conditions indicated.

We are for the political unity of the working class. Therefore, we are ready to collaborate most closely with all Social-Democrats who are for the united front and sincerely support unity on the above-mentioned principles.

But precisely because we are for unity, we shall struggle resolutely against all "Left" demagogues who try to make use of the disillusionment of the Social Democratic workers to create new Socialist Parties or Internationals directed against the Communist movement, and thus keep deepening the split in the working class.

We welcome the growing efforts among Social-Democratic workers for a united front with the Communists. In this fact we see a growth of their revolutionary consciousness and a beginning of the healing of the split in the working class. Being of the opinion that unity of action is a pressing necessity and the truest road to the establishment of the political unity of the proletariat as well, we declare that the Communist International and its sections are ready to enter into negotiations with the Second International and its sections for the establishment of the unity of the working class in the struggle against the offensive of capital, against fascism and the menace of an imperialist war.

Conclusion

Comrades, I am concluding my report. As you see, taking into account the change in the situation since the Sixth Congress and the lessons of our struggle, and relying on the degree of consolidation already achieved, we are raising a number of questions today in a new way, primarily the question of the united front and of the approach to Social-Democracy, the reformist trade unions and other mass organizations.

There are wiseacres who will sense in all this a digression from our basic positions, some sort of turn to the Right from the straight line of Bolshevism. Well, in my country, Bulgaria, they say that a hungry hen always dreams of millet. Let those political chickens think so.

This interests us little. For it is important that our own Parties and the broad masses throughout the world should correctly understand what we are striving for.

We would not be revolutionary Marxists, Leninists, worthy pupils of Marx, Engels, and Lenin, if we did not suitably *reconstruct* our policies and tactics in accordance with the changing situation and the changes occurring in the world labor movement.

We would not be real revolutionaries if we did not learn from our own experience and the experience of the masses.

We want our Parties in the capitalist countries to come out and act as *real political parties of the working class*, to become in actual fact a *political factor* in the life of their countries, to pursue at all times *an active Bolshevik mass policy and not confine themselves to propaganda and criticism, and bare appeals to struggle for a proletarian dictatorship.*

We are *enemies of all cut-and-dried schemes.* We want to take into account the concrete situation at each moment, in each place, and not act according to *a fixed, stereotyped form* anywhere and everywhere, not to forget that in *varying* circumstances the position of the Communists cannot be *identical.*

We want soberly to take into account all stages in the development of the class struggle and in the growth of the class consciousness of the masses themselves, to be able to locate and solve at each stage the *concrete* problems of the revolutionary movement corresponding to this stage.

We want to find a *common language* with the broadest masses for the purpose of struggling against the class enemy, to find ways of finally overcoming *the isolation of the revolutionary vanguard* from the masses of the proletariat and all other working people, as well as of overcoming the fatal *isolation of the working class itself from* its natural allies in the struggle against the bourgeoisie, against fascism.

We want to draw increasingly wide masses into the revolutionary class struggle and lead them to the proletarian revolution *proceeding from their vital interests and needs as the starting point, and their own experience as the basis.*

Following the example of our glorious Russian Bolsheviks, the example of the leading party of the Communist International, the Communist Party of the Soviet Union, we want to combine *the revolutionary heroism* of the German, the Spanish, the Austrian and other Communists with *genuine revolutionary realism,* and put an end to the last remnants of scholastic tinkering with serious political questions.

We want to equip our Parties from every angle for the solution of the highly complex political problems confronting them. For this purpose we want to raise ever higher their *theoretical level*, to train them in the spirit of living Marxism-Leninism and not fossilized doctrinairism.

We want to eradicate from our ranks all *self-satisfied sectarianism*, which above all blocks our road to the masses and impedes the carrying out of a truly Bolshevik mass policy.

We want to intensify in every way the struggle against concrete manifestations of Right opportunism, bearing in mind that the danger from this side will arise precisely in the course of carrying out our mass policy and struggle.

We want the Communists of every country promptly to draw and apply *all the lessons* that can be drawn from their own experience as the revolutionary vanguard of the proletariat. We want them *as quickly as possible to learn how to sail on the turbulent waters of the class struggle*, and not to remain on the shore as observers and registrars of the surging waves in the expectation of fine weather.

This is what we want.

And we want all this because only in this way will the working class at the head of all the working people, welded into a million-strong revolutionary army, led by the Communist International, be able to fulfil its historical mission with certainty -- to sweep fascism off the face of the earth and, together with it, capitalism!

(At the close of the report all delegates joined in a lengthy ovation, cheering enthusiastically and singing the revolutionary songs of their countries.)

NOTES

1. *Moratorium* -- A deferment, or suspension of payment, usually under extraordinary circumstances, such as war pestilence, natural calamities, etc. Hitler, to win over the middle and small peasant masses, proclaimed a moratorium of their debts to the state at the very beginning of his rule, but failed to fulfil his promise.

2. *Tsarist Okhrana* -- Gendarme institution in Tsarist Russia, set up at the Police Department in 1881 to combat the revolutionary movement, dissolved during the February Bourgeois Democratic Revolution in 1917.

3. In the autumn of 1922, the reactionary government of Seipel, President of the Christian-Social Party and agent of big business, the landowners and the Vatican, concluded a pact with the German National Party for the establishment of a government of the so-called anti-Marxist front, which would comprise all the reactionary forces in the struggle against the workers' movement.

4. Referring to the program adopted by the Congress of the Social-Democratic Party in Linz.

5. *Schutzbund* -- Social-Democratic para-military organization in Austria.

6. The Social-Democratic Government of Braun and Severing ruled Prussia from 1920 to 1932, pursuing a policy inimical to the Communist Party and the working masses, suppressing the Red Front mass organization, using police force to smash every action of the proletariat and forming an armed force of the bourgeoisie. When von Papen organized a coup d'état in Prussia in July 1932, overthrowing the Social-Democratic Government, Braun and Severing, although they had armed forces at their disposal, ignominiously capitulated together with the other leaders of the German Social-Democratic party.

7. *Reichsbanner* -- 'Union of the Imperial Banner', para-military Social-Democratic mass organization in Germany.

8. On the pretext that a 'second revolution' for the overthrow of Hitler was being prepared, on the eve of June 30, 1934, the entire leadership of the SA organization of storm troops was arrested and its chief commanders, including Minister Röhm, who headed the SA, were shot on the spot. The operation was conducted under the personal direction of Hitler in München and of Göring in Berlin. Several thousand commanders were arrested, and the SA was temporarily dissolved, to be radically purged and reorganized. Hitler was forced to this measure under the direct pressure of big business, so as to put an end to the demagogic propaganda of a 'second revolution' and to destroy its petty bourgeois advocates among the SA.

9. *Stronnictwo Ludowe* (People's Party) -- A democratic agrarian party in Poland, defending the interests mainly of the well-to-do peasants, headed the general strike of the peasant masses in August 1937 under the pressure of the local peasants' organizations.

10. *Kraft durch Freude* (Strength through Joy) -- A mass fascist organization in Nazi Germany, aimed at the fascization of workers and their training for future soldiers.

11. *Dopo lavoro* -- 'After work' -- organization in Italy similar to *Kraft durch Freude*.

12. *De Man* -- One of the leaders of the Social-Democratic Party in Belgium, on whose orders he drafted in 1933 the so-called 'Plan of de Man', envisaging a 'peaceful transition to socialism', which was adopted as the official party program at the end of 1933.

13. The National-Liberation Alliance -- A mass antifascist organization formed at the beginning of 1935 in Brazil by progressive political parties and organizations headed by the Communist Party, defeated in an armed struggle against reaction in November 1935.